PRAYER WITHOUT PRETENDING

Prayer without Pretending

*What Happens When We Pray Through
Guilt, Hurt, Shame, and Confusion*

Angela Ashwin

Servant Publications
Ann Arbor, Michigan

Copyright © Angela Ashwin 1990
All rights reserved.

First American edition in 1991.

Published by Servant Publications
P.O. Box 8617
Ann Arbor, Michigan 48107

Cover design by Michael Andaloro
91 92 93 94 95   10 9 8 7 6 5 4 3 2 1

Printed in the United States of America
ISBN 0-89283-698-9

Library of Congress Cataloging-in-Publication Data

Ashwin, Angela.
  Prayer without pretending / what happens when we pray
through guilt, hurt, shame, and confusion / Angela Ashwin.—
1st American ed.
        p.   cm.
Includes bibliographical references.
ISBN 0-89283-698-9
1. Prayer.   I. Title.
BV215.A84   1991
248.3'2—dc20

91-11614

For Vincent

Contents

Part Two: Praying with Your Sinfulness

Part Three: Praying with Misfortunes, Fears, and Frustrations

Preface

I COULD NOT HAVE WRITTEN THIS BOOK ON MY OWN. As well as writing out of my own struggle to pray when things have been hard, I have drawn on the experience and insights of friends, and of others whose words I have read or heard.

I can only thank a few people by name: Sister Rosemary, SLG, for her wise comments, Anne Haire and Mary Tomkinson, who have helped me enormously in the sections about illness, and members of the women's group at St. Agnes' Church, Burmantofts, Leeds, who used Parts 1 and 2 of this book as a basis for discussion. I particularly value the feedback from Pippa Julings and Liz Schweiger.

I must also thank John White for his poem *Who Shakes a Fist at God*, and many other friends for their quiet and prayerful encouragement during these months of writing.

My children have been marvelously patient, frequently putting up with a harassed and preoccupied mother. I am especially grateful to my husband, Vincent, both for his unflagging support, and for his perceptive criticisms and suggestions about the text.

Unless otherwise stated, biblical quotations are from the *Revised Standard Version*, Second Edition, 1971, and quotations from the Psalms come from *The Alternative Service Book* (SPCK 1980).

Some ideas in this book appeared originally in a series of

articles which I wrote for the magazine *Christian* (published by Marshall Pickering), between May 1987 and November 1988.

Introduction

Jesus did not come to explain suffering, nor to take it away; he came to fill it with his presence. **Paul Claudel**[1]

PRAYER IS TURNING OUR WHOLE BEING TO GOD, and staying there. The trouble is that all sorts of things seem to spoil our attempts to pray, or even prevent us from praying at all. You could call them our "if only's":

"If only I weren't so pressed for time…"

"If only so-and-so were not so impossible…"

"If only I didn't feel so tired… *then* I could pray."

We wish we could jump over the fence, out of our own plot of grass and onto the next, as if our spiritual life would suddenly become greener on the other side. We are missing the fact that God wants us where we are, here and now.

We need to turn "if only" firmly on its head, and say, "Only this, only now: this is where I will meet God."

It doesn't matter how unsatisfactory or chaotic our lives are; prayer is still possible, because God is not waiting for us to become "worthy" of a spiritual life or expert in its techniques. He simply asks us to open ourselves to him, so that he can be given space to love the confused, selfish person we are. That is what prayer is about: God's love for us, and our response to that love—not our own so-called spiritual achievements.

If we are honest, we will realize that we can be so preoccupied or distracted during prayer that it seems we aren't praying at all. But the fact that prayer can be difficult doesn't mean that it is hypocritical to read a book like this, or that the kind of prayer I am exploring is beyond ordinary people who have ordinary problems and bad moods.

Often, prayer simply consists of bringing God the things that have been happening over the last few hours or days, during which we may hardly have given him a thought. The last thing we should do is say to ourselves, "I've been letting prayer slip, so there's no point in starting now." There is every reason for praying now: God wants us as we are, not as we think we ought to be.

If we attempt to pray when we are miserable or angry, we can find it difficult to concentrate. Familiar patterns of confession, thanksgiving, praise, and meditation seem lifeless. Again, that does not matter. Praying is not an activity which depends on our skill, like swimming or cooking. Prayer involves coming to God as we are, with our pain, distraction, ill temper, and all.

Everything is raw material for prayer, including the darkest parts of our lives. Even our worst emotions can become prayer's content, prayer's pain, prayer's energy, and prayer's joke. Far worse than making a mess of prayer is giving up praying altogether.

This is not to decry the more traditional forms of spirituality. If our lives are going to be rooted in God, we do need some sort of basic pattern of prayer, however often we break it. (The way we work this out in practice will vary according to our circumstances and personalities.) But prayer does not have to end when we finish our "quiet time." It can permeate all of life, including the weary and unhappy parts of it.

PROTEST AND SAY YES

It seems a contradiction to say that we should both protest and say yes to God when painful things come our way. But that is the paradox of prayer. Protesting alone could leave us in a vacuum, with nothing other than our misery to hang on to. Just saying yes, on the other hand, could lead to a false piety, where we repressed our true feelings and meekly accepted everything unjust and unpleasant as though it were "the will of God."

We need *both* the freedom to explode to God, *and* the courage to accept the truth of what is happening to us.

People sometimes see prayer *only* in terms of complaining to God about their problems and asking him to take them away. If he doesn't provide instant relief, they decide that prayer is not worth the trouble.

But asking for help is only the beginning of prayer, not its end. If God does not immediately remove our difficulties, we have to find a way of working through them; this is where the mysterious business of saying yes to God begins. We do not have to pretend that we feel fine when we do not; nor do we need to resign ourselves to the arbitrary whims of a tyrant god. What we are asked to do is turn toward God from the middle of our pain and confusion, and say yes to whatever he will do in and through the situation.

It is precisely the discomfort of this sort of prayer that makes it so real. The fact that we are sometimes hurt or anxious brings us close to Christ in his suffering. As Christians, we are called to face our own pain, and the pain of the world, and to hold the whole mess in the powerful love of the crucified and risen Christ, to be healed and redeemed by him.

THIS IS NOT A HANDBOOK OF EASY ANSWERS

People are mysterious beings. You can fix a broken leg or arm, but you cannot "solve" a person's grief or pain. You can analyze humans as a collection of bodily cells consisting mostly of water, or as a sociological phenomenon, with an average of two-and-a-half children and one-fifth of a nervous breakdown per head. But you cannot sum up a whole person in any set of statistics.

Really to know an individual means entering the mysterious world of love and vulnerability and laughter. Whatever we long for and suffer and create are what make us who we are, as unique human beings; these things cannot be quantified.

The closer you are to a person, the more you realize that there is still a vast area inside the person that you hardly touch. We cannot even know ourselves fully, or begin to plumb the depths of our own subconscious. Hurt, guilt, and fear are part of this mysterious side of our human nature, and praying with these things will not provide clear-cut solutions or techniques guaranteed to remove the pain.

The experience of suffering is part of being alive in a world where fun, unselfishness, and beauty are mixed up with sickening cruelty and devastating disasters. Prayer is not an escape route from the shadows; it is a way of facing them with God.

READING THIS BOOK

There are various ways in which this book could be used. The individual sections within each part are deliberately short, so that busy people can pick up and meditate on a section or two at available moments. You might want to read the book in short doses, perhaps taking one theme each day. At the end of each section reflections or quotations are provided to lead you into prayer. My own experience with books like this is that on some days I have a particular need, so that I only want to dip into certain parts. At other times I enjoy reading through larger sections of the book.

Our situations and personalities vary so much that ideas which strike one person will leave another cold. Our moods change, too, so that a suggestion which irritates someone on

Tuesday may be fairly helpful on Thursday. In the end it is God who guides us to pray, in the ways he wants.

* * *

Alone with God

Christian: *Lord, maybe I ought to do some penance or fasting; my life's such a mess.*

God: *You've got enough difficulty to contend with already; work through that with me before you think about piling any other uncomfortable things onto yourself.*

Christian: *Lord, I can't do any spiritual exercises until I've got my own problems out of the way.*

God: *But your problems are your spiritual exercises. So let's get on with it!*

Part One

Praying with Your Hurts

Jesus' ordinary, everyday clothes shone, the clothes of work and sweat and travel; his ordinary body was transfigured, the body prone to weariness and pain, and destined to suffer much more.

The same is true for us in prayer.

Maria Boulding,
writing about the
Transfiguration of Jesus [1]

ONE

He Took Bread

The nagging pain we experience when somebody has hurt us can threaten to swamp our feelings and spoil everything we do. Yet a turning point comes if we can take the pain in both hands and face it, instead of running away from it or letting it overwhelm us.

SEVERAL YEARS AGO, I had an experience which changed the way I prayed. I was hurt and angry. Some unkind things were being said about me, and I had just heard about a particularly nasty bit of gossip on my way to church. It was the last straw. As I entered church, tears welled up in my eyes. I tried to pray, but I was full of resentment. During the communion service, familiar words hit me like a bomb:

"On the night that Jesus was betrayed, he took bread."

He took bread!

Jesus took hold of the bread of his suffering, grasping his own agonizing situation, and transformed it into a supremely life-giving and healing act.

"This is my body, broken for you...."

At that moment I began to see that there were new possibilities for praying with my own anger and misery.

Until then, I had always allowed my hurt feelings to dominate me. But now I realized that I no longer needed to remain the victim of someone else's wrongdoing. Instead, I could take hold of my pain, just as Jesus had taken hold of the bread.

But could I really do it? I wasn't sure I could summon the strength. Then something else occurred to me. Jesus had already taken hold of my pain, and received it into himself on the cross. I was not alone in this, and God was not expecting me to perform some impossible spiritual feat. He was simply asking if I was willing to try to face my hurt, with him.

"ACCEPTING" IS A DANGEROUS WORD

To say that praying with pain involves facing and accepting the hard things could be misunderstood as mindless submission:

"Let your drunk husband hit you...."

"Don't try to stop people taking advantage of you...."

"You've just got to put up with oppression!"

But the sort of acceptance that Christ taught us involves standing firm against what is wrong, both in ourselves and others, while taking the responsibility that our situation demands.

I know of a couple who adopted two infants from Bangladesh. At first, certain racially prejudiced members of their own family were highly indignant, and neighbors even snubbed them on the street. "Acceptance" for this couple did not mean feebly giving in to the pressure of their opponents; it meant being prepared to resist people's opposition and to take the sting of racist remarks, as an unavoidable part of being mom and dad to those babies. Theirs was an act of strength, not weakness, and they depended constantly on God in order to keep going.

Facing and accepting our problems may actually increase

the pain at first. But the only alternative is to run away from ourselves and God.

One Bible study group I know of decided to discuss the points about bread and suffering in their small group meeting. Members shared honestly and deeply about their own experiences of hurt. Afterwards, they used some bread as a symbol to help bring their prayer alive. Later, the leader of the group wrote to me:

It was a particularly potent image for us to see the piece of bread as representing our *own* hurt. I led with the words: "As we share the bread and pass it around, let us see in it our own brokenness. Let us take it in both hands, hold it, face it, and remember that Jesus took his broken life into his hands too."

From something as ordinary as bread, he saw his mission in a new light—the bread had to be broken before it could be life-giving.

Let us offer our lives, as they are, to be taken up into Christ's suffering love in the world.

* * *

Thank you, Lord, that you understand our emotions and weaknesses better than we do. Thank you for showing us how your brokenness has become the way to new life and healing.

TWO

We Need to Get Angry

Some people are cautious about giving vent to their hurt and bitterness in prayer, because it seems disrespectful to tell God that you can't stand somebody. Yet we need an outlet for our feelings. Prayer offers the supreme opportunity for this, if we have the courage to give God and then stay with him, so that our anger and pain can be redeemed.

I T IS IMMENSELY FRUSTRATING not to be allowed to cry about things, or to express what we really feel. Logical arguments about why we should not be upset only make matters worse. We need to express our hurts with someone who loves us, with someone who won't simply tell us that we ought to pull ourselves together.

If this is true on a human level, it applies even more in our relationship with God. When we release our true feelings to God, anger and all, his grace and love begin to break in.

The problem is that this approach seems irreverent. "You can't say things like that to God!" exclaimed one woman during a discussion about praying with hurts. "You should confess the fact that you feel angry, but that's all!"

I understand what she means, and I share her desire to give the best we can to God. But I know that if I did not tell God exactly what I thought, I would be hiding something

7

from him. God does not wait until we are purified of all our rottenness before we can approach him. He wants us as we are, and offers us the freedom to be totally ourselves with him. He knows what is going on inside us anyway, so why try to hold back from him the very things that most need healing?

If we try to avoid life's difficulties, or eliminate them from our prayer, they will ultimately increase their hold on us. Bottled-up emotions invariably backfire later on, when they can wreak emotional havoc. They may surface in some form of depression, or in a smoldering resentment which later results in vindictive outbursts against other people.

Another reason why people are afraid to express their anger to God is that it could seem to be justifying bitterness and resentment. But God will not spoil us or encourage us to be petty and vindictive, as an overindulgent parent would. We can trust him to make us the person we were created to be, however painful the purifying process. Pouring out our anger to God reduces its power and clears the air, so that we can then move on to something deeper.

Sometimes people find it helpful to write down their grievances, and then literally hold the paper up to Christ, as a prayer for help and forgiveness.

While we are right in the midst of irritating or hurtful circumstances, a helpful way to pray is simply to use a short phrase, such as, "Lord, this is yours," or "Abba, Father," repeated many times. That may be the only sort of prayer that is real at this stage.

Once we have calmed down, we may be able to pray more reflectively about the situation, and perhaps view things from the other person's standpoint. We may also be able to see our troubles in wider perspective, as part of the pain of the world. But first we must be free enough to be angry.

* * *

The writers of the Psalms also exploded at times!

Contend, O Lord, with those who contend with me;
*   fight against those who fight against me!...*
But at my stumbling they gathered in glee...
*   gnashing at me with their teeth....*
Let not those rejoice over me
*   who are wrongfully my foes,*
and let not those wink the eye
*   who hate me without cause....*
They open wide their mouths against me;
*   they say, "Aha, aha!..."*
Thou hast seen, O Lord; be not silent!
*   O Lord, be not far from me!*
Bestir thyself, and awake for my right.... **Psalm 35:1, 15-16, 19, 21-23**

THREE

Something Hard to Carry

Persistent domestic problems can make it very difficult for us to pray—at least in an ordered and peaceful way. Even if we do manage to pray through a painful clash, we still have to face the person we find difficult, and then it seems that the irritation and conflict begin all over again.

It seems an endless process of getting hurt and struggling to cope. We may be tempted to stop praying entirely. Forgiveness seems beyond us, we are ashamed of our self-pitying reactions, and feel that we simply cannot be ourselves....

The turning point comes when we can see things from a different perspective.

JIM AND MARGOT WERE GOING THROUGH A ROUGH TIME in the middle years of their marriage. Margot was unwell, and had become increasingly tense and irritable. She criticized Jim's efforts to help her at home, but complained that she had too much housework to do. She often interpreted innocent remarks as personal criticisms, and accused family members of ganging up against her. She wanted as much pity as possible from everybody, so she told her friends a lot of half-truths about Jim, making it seem as though he didn't care about her.

Jim wondered how much longer he could stand it. His peace with God was shattered, and he felt increasingly guilty about the resentment building inside him. In desperation he went to see an old friend and told him what was happening.

After a pause the older man said, "Tell me exactly what you want to do when she's at her worst."

"I want to shout at her, 'Go to hell, stew in your own juice—I'm leaving!'" Jim replied. "I would love to say it, just to relieve my own feelings. But I don't really want to do that to her. I could never just pack my bags and go."

"Okay, so that's your immediate reaction. Now consider whether you can put into words what you want for Margot, deep down."

Jim replied slowly, "I suppose I want the best for her; I want her to be herself again, to be happy."

"And that's going to take a lot of healing," continued the older man, "plus a good deal of praying. I think God is asking you to share with him the painful burden of what's going on in Margot. She's all knotted up inside, and every time she hurts you, she is passing on to you a bit of herself which needs healing. You're being given something to carry—like a piece of wood—and it's for her sake.

"When she starts being unkind again, a bit of Margot is coming hurtling across at you, almost like a parcel flying through the air, and landing—womph—in your lap. It hurts, but don't let the pain sour you; see if you can grasp hold of it as a positive act, something you do, as well as something done to you.

"It's as if God were saying, 'Here, will you carry this... for Margot?'

"Let's face it, sometimes you'll be so angry you will simply want to rebel and shout no at God. Go ahead and let him know how you feel. Don't try to hide anything from him.

"But at other times I think you will manage to say yes, though it will take all your strength, and you may wonder how it can possibly be of any use. I think that the only prayer being asked of you at the moment is to work it all through with God."

* * *

Eternal life is found not by those who seek the heroic cross, but by those who do not dodge the humdrum one. Fison[2]

FOUR

People Who Bring Out the Worst in Us

Clashes with difficult people bring out unpleasant elements in our own personality, aspects of ourselves that we would rather not acknowledge. But even self-pity and hostility can be grist for the mill of prayer.

A N IRRITATING THING ABOUT PEOPLE who are always finding fault is that there is usually some truth to what they say. Perhaps we *have* been unwise or forgetful; maybe we *are* inefficient at times. But what hurts and fills us with self-pity is the way people stand in judgment of us, evident by their unending list of comments or criticism, veiled or otherwise.

When we are blamed or attacked by someone, our first instinct is to leap to our own defense. Before we know what has happened, we've hurt the other person back. Afterwards we chide ourselves for losing our temper, and wonder with dismay how much insecurity and selfishness remains in us to be healed and forgiven.

In certain relationships, we may become oversensitive, exasperating our friends by sensing criticism even when it was not intended.

TWO FIRES

Two kinds of fire can burn inside us. One is a smoldering fire of resentment, which flares up at any moment and does far more damage to us than to the person who is hurting us. We brood on the insult, justifying ourselves, indulging in numerous daydreams in which we get even with those who hurt us.

The other kind of fire is difficult to kindle by ourselves, but God can kindle it in us when we pray. It is a purifying fire which consumes our self-centeredness, and clears enough space for us to be able to admit our mistakes. We encounter a sense of freedom, almost lightness of spirit when we can see beyond our blistering indignation to the things that we need to watch in ourselves.

God is not a faultfinder; he harbors no mean or vindictive thoughts against us. So there is nothing to fear in facing our faults with him.

We still wince when the next tirade of blame comes: "Here we go again," we think to ourselves, "now what have I done?" We may have to pray through this pain many times if a relationship continues to be problematic. But such pain isn't necessarily bad, especially if it helps us see what needs to change in us. Dark sides of our nature are surfacing which might never otherwise have been opened up to God, for him to redeem and transform.

* * *

Lord, I thank you that you understand me totally.
Burn away the resentment in me.
You know how unkind and unjust the things are which have
*   been said.*

Help me to see clearly which aspects of my own behavior I
  should look at as well.
Am I prepared to expose my weaknesses to you, honestly?
Lord, use the pain to purge away a bit more of my pride.

"To be redeemed from fire, by fire." T.S. Eliot [3]

FIVE

The Pain of Criticism

"Reputation" is a particularly heavy piece of luggage to carry around, and it is good to be free of it. Ideally we should be able to travel light with both praise and blame, but that is easier said than done.

M OST PEOPLE FEEL UNEASY when others disapprove of them or of their opinions. We want to be liked and accepted, and most of us tend to assume that we have a right to be completely understood, always and everywhere. In fact, such understanding is a luxury, which we will only occasionally enjoy.

We may be so obsessed with preserving an untarnished reputation that we become like a circus-artist, frantically dashing around keeping numerous plates spinning on rods. But we must stop trying to please everybody.

Imagine a scenario in which you were anything but unpopular. Suppose everybody worshiped the ground you walked on! Would you really be happy? I doubt it.

Praying through criticism offers an opportunity to ask God to prune us of our pride. Many of us still go red in the face when people disagree with us, especially in public. And we have only to be the butt of an unfair remark for a wave of indignation to sweep over us once more.

It will help if we can see the funny side of our desire to present an absolutely perfect image to the world. The fact that we dislike being misunderstood should not, however, make us feel guilty. It is natural to feel that way. The question is really about our priorities. Does our concern for approval take up too much of our attention, and overrule other, more important things? When we realize how infinitely we are loved by God, our craving to be loved and accepted by other people becomes less vital. This is one of the many reasons why prayer helps.

HORATIO

I have a name for my fear of disapproval: "Horatio." When I start worrying about what people think of me, I can say to myself, "Now then, Horatio! I know you!"

Horatio is a comic character, a pompous ass strutting around the stage. He fusses and flaps when he thinks he might be offending anybody, and will drop hints about an easy way out if any conflict appears on the horizon.

Trying to bully old Horatio into submission doesn't work; he always pops up again. It is better to laugh at him along with God (in other words, to laugh at yourself), putting him in perspective next to the infinite stature of Christ. Then the huffing and puffing Horatio will be cut down to size.

Through prayer, God makes our Horatios harmless, loving them out of existence, and giving us courage to be ourselves.

* * *

God looks at each of us with the eyes of love. Other people look at us with their own particular squint, and often have only a partial understanding of who we are.

God knows us,
God accepts us, as we really are,
God forgives us,
God loves us. That is what matters.

"Spirituality is not concerned with our defenses, but with their removal." **Alan Ecclestone**[4]

SIX

Irritation—
A Yes Which Hurts

*Few emotions threaten to sabotage our prayer as efficiently
as irritation. Somehow we have to find a way of bringing
our irritated feelings into prayer, so that they can become
something constructive.*

THE FOLLOWING FICTIONAL STORY illustrates the problem.
David got up early, and went into the living room to
have a time of quiet with God before going to work. The
room smelled awful; a stray cat must have come in through
the cat-flap during the night. David remembered the previ-
ous evening's conversation: his wife had wanted to leave the
entry open because the cat was out, and it was frosty. He
had warned her that there was a stray cat in the yard, but to
no avail.

He shouted upstairs, "I knew this would happen; there's
a foul smell of cat down here!"

A voice emerged from the bathroom, "Sorry" (her tone of
voice clearly indicating that she didn't mean it). "Anyway,
you should have shut the inside kitchen door." Slam!

Increasing irritation took over as David tried to pray. He
attempted to concentrate on a passage from Jeremiah, but

23

the smell nauseated him. So he decided to give up and go for a walk, praying as he went. But still the irritation lingered.

Sometimes our irritation is quite unjustified; we are bothered because someone sniffs too frequently, or moves too slowly, or squeezes the tube of toothpaste at the wrong end. At other times we are irritated over things which are genuinely wrong: when people don't do their fair share of work or when they constantly leave the house a mess.

However justified our feelings may or may not be, the irritation that surges over us still has to be handled. How do we pray with it? We might try reading the Bible, only to find that it is impossible to concentrate or that the passage we are reading seems irrelevant to our concerns.

Stop a minute and ask yourself why you are so rattled. What is it that matters so much to you, to have disrupted your inner peace?

This can be a revealing exercise. All kinds of things may have been spoiled or threatened by the other person. Your concern might be a selfish one, such as your routine being disrupted or your reputation as a homemaker questioned. Or you might be concerned about the well-being of a friend or the aims of a movement you support.

Suppose you are irritated because a friend is ill and her family has not bothered to visit her, even though they live nearby. Or suppose you wrote to the local newspaper about a question of injustice and they only printed half your letter, so that you appeared to be saying the opposite of what you meant.

In such situations, your irritation can be made into a prayer, a "yes" to those things which matter: your friend's welfare, the justice issue. Sometimes the pain of irritation is simply the cost of caring.

Other causes which have burned so fiercely in us will

cease to be so important to us when we expose them to the light of God. Is it really so vital who gets the first cup of coffee at the office or how short or long our children's hair is? Does it matter that our public image is affected? A "yes" to God in these circumstances is not easy. It is a "yes" to the dent in our pride and comfort, a "yes" to the irritation itself.

We don't like it; but facing irritation this way can be a kind of purification, so that we become a fraction more like the loving, self-forgetful person we were meant to be.

Maybe it's Saturday, a rare opportunity to sleep late. But the phone rings early in the morning and wakes you up. How do you pray with your irritation?

Ask yourself what matters so much to you. Is it your need of sleep? Perhaps. But what about the person who woke you up? Can you say yes to her, accepting her as she is, or do you expect her to be perfect? God accepts you constantly, as you are, with all your irritating and selfish habits. Are you tempted to be like the servant in the parable in Matthew 18:23-35, refusing to forgive somebody this one tiny thing, when you are yourself forgiven so much? Do you only accept people on certain conditions?

You will probably want to mention this incident to her, and ask her to call a bit later on Saturdays. But, for the present, you are asked to take on board the chafing irritation inside you. As well as protesting, you must also say yes in this costly business of loving.

Let's return to the cat-beleaguered husband. What matters most?

A pleasant, sweet-smelling home?

The desire to establish that he was right and his wife wrong?

Accepting that his wife is human and sometimes makes mistakes of judgment?

Accepting her?

* * *

"Prayer is the battlefield in which we conquer by letting God conquer." S. Kierkegaard (1813-1855)

The following prayer calls on Christ for help:
Come, my Light, and illuminate my darkness.
Come, my Life, and revive me from death.
Come, my Physician, and heal my wounds.
Come, Flame of divine love, and burn up the thorns of
    my sins,
Kindling my heart with the flame of thy love...
For Thou alone art my King and my Lord.

St. Dimitri of Rostrov (17th century)[5]

SEVEN

Outrage

*How do you pray when you return home from a vacation
to find your house broken into and ransacked? Most of us
would say, "You don't!" But after we have raged at everyone and everything, and sorted out some of the chaos, we
may calm down sufficiently to ponder in prayer what our
possessions mean to us.*

YOU FEEL VIOLATED when you find that burglars have been
through all your belongings, especially if they've damaged or stolen articles which were especially meaningful to
you.

"Prayer?" you utter in amazement. "You must be joking!"

But I'm not. Don't be afraid to get angry in front of God.
Tell him exactly how you feel about it. If you hang on to
your anger and nurse it, the devil has won. You are letting
what happened poison you. Pour out your fury to God for
as long as you need to. This is a time when accepting the situation means putting feelings into words. Later on, other
ways of praying may be possible, because having your
house broken into can help you realize what really matters
to you.

Losing something given to you by somebody you care
about is part of the pain of loving; can you make your pain a
"yes" to that love? Losing your VCR is an irritation, but it

wouldn't have happened if you didn't have the luxury of possessing such a marvelous gadget. Can you turn your loss into a prayer of "yes" to the huge privilege and responsibility of being a first-class passenger on this planet?

TO PONDER

* Before I was born, my clothes, meals, name, and living place were all decided for me, and I entered this world with empty hands and a good deal of indignity.
* When I die people will go through all my belongings anyway, possibly with respect, possibly not.
* How much do I depend on my possessions and my dignity? Am I willing to ask God to make me more detached, and therefore more free?
* My possessions are not me; people can violate my house, but they cannot violate me unless I let them.
* To imagine that I have absolute power over my things or my fortune is an illusion, as I discover only too well when my wallet is stolen or illness wrecks my plans.

The rich landowner in Jesus' parable realized too late how futile it had been to put all his security into barns full of hoarded goods. He had said to himself, "'Soul, you have ample goods laid up for many years; take your ease, eat, drink, be merry.' But God said to him, 'Fool! This night your soul is required of you; and the things you have prepared, whose will they be?'" (Luke 12:16-20).

The more I let go, the less I have to lose. Nobody can take from me the things that really matter.

* * *

Lord Jesus,
I give you my hands to do your work.
I give you my feet to go your way.

I give you my mouth to speak your words.
I give you my mind that you may think in me.
I give you my goods that you may share through me.
And I give you my spirit that you may pray in me,
so that it is you, Lord,
who live and move and have your being in me. Amen.

Based on a prayer in a sixteenth-century Book of Hours

EIGHT

Deep Wounds

What do you do with the feelings you have about someone who deliberately works against you out of jealousy and spite, or who is openly vindictive toward you or grossly dishonest behind your back? Trying to pray at such times can involve a long, hard night of the spirit. As well as working through our reactions, both worthy and unworthy, we need to face a crucial question: do we want hatred to dominate the way we live from now on?

A DEEP HURT CAN INFLICT AN OPEN SORE which refuses to heal. In such a condition, we hardly feel like loving the person who has wounded us. Perhaps the only honest prayer we can muster is, "Oh God, I hate that person. Forgive me." Once we have expressed our feelings to God, we can ask him for help. And that help often comes in the form of a question: "Do you want to hate that person above all else?"

"Wanting-not-to hate" may be the nearest we can get to loving at this stage. It may not seem like much, but it is vital. That tiny spark of desire against the power of hatred is the work of the Holy Spirit in us, however muffled and disguised it may be.

If we offer the whole mixed bag of our desires and emotions to God, he will help us to sift out the more selfish side of our nature, which simply wants revenge, from that of our better self.

When someone's unkindness seems too much to bear, try lighting a candle when you pray. The flame can symbolize your deeper desire that your anger will be purged by God's fire of love, in spite of considerable surface resentment.

In cases where we've been wronged, we aren't likely to take care of the problem in one neat attempt. Waves of hatred may keep coming over us, especially if the hurtful person goes on to inflict fresh wounds. Our feelings have to be offered to God again and again, often with tears and even a sense of despair.

But Christ is with us in this darkness. Absolutely nothing can separate us from his love. When he rose from the dead and appeared to the disciples, he did not have a totally other-worldly body, untouched by the pain of human life. Jesus was still wounded, and made a point of showing those wounds to the disciples (Luke 24:39; John 20:27).

He still bears those marks today, with us and for us, and when we pray with our hurts we can place our wounds in his. This is not easy, and it is right to be suspicious of easy platitudes about "radiant sufferers" or "pain made easy." What does matter is that we keep on bringing everything to Jesus.

For some people, a way of praying with pain is to go through and beyond it into silence. If someone has wronged you, picture the hurt still thrashing around inside you like a spiked wheel. From each spike fly out sparks of rage and anger, words of self-pity, words of revenge, words of self-justification. Imagine the spiked wheel gradually slowing down and stopping. Let your pain become focused into a clear, single stab of pain. Face it; sit still with it.

Then hold the pain up to Christ in an offering without words. Imagine his pain on the cross. By doing this you give him the whole package, your wounds and your own failings. It is his pain as well as yours.

There is a silence in the heart of suffering. Stay there in the stillness, vulnerable and exposed, so that the pain becomes the point where God touches you most deeply.

* * *

I will face this,
I will accept its full impact, silently turning my gaze onto the
crucified Christ,
who is in the darkness with me,
I am enfolded and held in the love of God
who is both Love-in-death and Love-Risen.

NINE

A Vital Link in Forgiveness

There is a strange link between us and the person hurting us, which puts us in a unique position to pray for that one. Forgiving also brings us closer to God himself.

I ULIA DE BEAUSOBRE was a Russian Christian who was imprisoned in the 1930s after the Bolshevik revolution. She said that whenever she was being tortured, she had a curious sense of being closer to her torturer than anyone else in the world. On the receiving end of such a stream of cruelty from him, she was in direct contact with the evil inside him, and could therefore pray for him at a very deep level. She also knew that the pain was shared by Christ, and felt a strong sense of "participation" with him in the "suffering and the redeeming of the deed."[6]

Such heroism is beyond most of us. Yet Iulia's story is a parable illustrating a mysterious fact. We have a unique opportunity to pray for the healing of a person who wrongs us, because our hurt has opened up a direct channel of contact between us. Our pain can be the point where God's love meets that person, through prayer. This is God's doing, not ours.

WHAT IS FORGIVENESS?

Forgiveness means poverty on our part and activity on God's. We have to let the pain carve out a channel in us, rather than cause a blockage. Dirt and rubbish accumulate in blocked pipes, so that a whole system is poisoned. But a hollowed-out channel allows God's energy of healing and reconciliation to be released.

Being hurt can fill us with bitterness; it can also clutter us up with self-righteousness. From our pedestal, we will condescend to pardon those who hurt us. Forgiveness, we suppose, is a thing that we will summon from our own resources, and graciously bestow on the guilty party—as long as they are duly penitent, of course.

But this is comic self-deception. True forgiveness means allowing the other person to be free, and letting go of our desire to extract the apology which we demand as our right. It means being sufficiently empty and "poor in spirit" to be a channel of God's gift of mercy, even when the wrong against us has not been redressed.

The following prayer was found in 1945 on a scrap of paper beside the dead body of a Jewish child in the Nazi concentration camp at Ravensbruck, where ninety-two thousand women and children died.

O Lord,
  remember not only the men and women of goodwill,
    but also those of ill will.
  But do not only remember the suffering they have
    inflicted upon us,
  remember the fruits we bought thanks to this suffering,
  our comradeship, our loyalty, our humility,
  the courage, the generosity,
  the greatness of heart which has grown out of all this.
  And when they come to judgment

let all the fruits that we have borne
be their forgiveness. Amen. Amen. Amen.[7]

* * *

In human life there is nothing more welcoming and
transparent to the presence of God than an attitude of forgiveness. It opens wide the gates for God. In forgiveness
God and human life touch, harmonize, melt together.
There the human being is in God's likeness, and a creator
with God.[8]

St. Stephen was in a unique position to pray for the Jews
of Jerusalem, because he was on the receiving end of their
malice.

As his fellow Jews were stoning Stephen, "he prayed,
'Lord Jesus, receive my spirit.' And he knelt down and cried
with a loud voice, 'Lord, do not hold this sin against them'"
(Acts 7:59-60).

TEN

Forgiving on Behalf of Others

Some people say that you cannot forgive those who hurt your friends, because that is your friends' job, not yours.

But to say that is an oversimplification. We belong to one another, and when somebody I love is hurt, I am hurt too. If I do not forgive, I will always be nursing bitterness on behalf of the person I love. That cannot be right.

It is not a matter of doing our friends' forgiving for them, in a crude exchange. We are called to pray for forgiveness with them and because of them; doing this can only help to release the healing power of God in them as well.

"I CAN FORGIVE THOSE WHO HURT ME, but not those who hurt my children." That's what many of us would say. It is certainly the greatest torture of all to witness cruelty inflicted on our family. Even comparatively minor hurts to our children can make us furious.

Some time ago I picked up my seven-year-old son, Andrew, from school, and took him to the drugstore to buy a candy bar for his father's birthday. I told him I would stand outside while he made the purchase, because I needed to watch for my daughter, who was coming home from a different school.

As I was coming out the door of the store, turning around to reassure Andrew that I would not be far away, a woman in a hurry pushed past me with a glare. Fair enough! I was in the way.

I waited and waited outside; the impatient lady came out again, followed by some teenagers. Still no Andrew.

Eventually he emerged in tears: "Mommy, the lady pushed in front of me, and then some girls did too. And I still haven't got Daddy's present."

I felt a wave of dislike for this woman; how dare she take advantage of *my son?* I was surprised by the strength of emotion which swept over me.

As I prayed through this later, two things stood out in my mind. *First,* by hurting Andrew, that lady had hurt me. To distinguish between hurting me and hurting someone I love would have been nonsense. When somebody else is wounded, I am wounded too. Whether I like it or not, I am involved with all those who are abused and oppressed, in the process of letting God's forgiveness into the matter. I cannot wash my hands of the situation, or say, "It's not for me to pray for the forgiveness of a corrupt politician or for drug kingpins who ruin the lives of our children." Each of us is caught up in the hurt and healing of the world.

Second, I knew I must do something with the disgust I felt. At least I could offer Jesus my anger over this small injustice and ask him to relieve those who suffer from the larger injustices of the world: for peasants struggling under tyrannical rulers; for families of hostages; or for refugees who watch as soldiers destroy food supplies that could save them and their children.

THE HARDER QUESTIONS

But what if your daughter has been raped by a man with AIDS? What if your child was run over by a drunk driver or your elderly parent mugged by a teenager? Can we presume to talk about forgiveness to people facing that sort of hell?

It would be cruel and insulting to say to them, "You really ought to forgive, you know." Such talk makes forgiveness sound like an achievement, produced by sheer willpower.

Forgiveness does *not* mean pretending that things don't hurt after all. It does not mean that we simply whitewash another's evil. At root, all forgiveness is God's gift; we are its channels, not its creators.

Somebody once asked me, "What would you say, as a Christian, to the parents of murdered children?"

With much fear and trembling, I would want to say: "I cannot imagine the depths of anguish you have gone through. But when things happen to hurt *my* children, they link me with you in a tiny way, so that I can offer my hurt to God for you.

"What can I say except that I hate what happened to your children, and grieve, and ask the question 'why?' with you? But I also reach out to God for healing of the terrible pain in you. When I try to forgive the people who hurt my children, I'm feeling what I'm feeling *for you* as well as for myself and my own family.

"I'm not saying that you ought to forgive; no one has the right to impose that on you from the outside. I stand empty-handed with you, praying for the power of God's love, instead of the hate which can destroy us both. All I have to offer you in the end is my weakness, and the fact that I care."

THE PARADOX

Can we hold in our hands anger and forgiveness at the same time?

I think we have to.

Forgiving someone who has harmed us or someone close to us, doesn't mean that we aren't angry about the wrong that was committed. But there are different kinds of anger. Smoldering resentment and a desire for revenge need to be purged and healed. But there is also a right kind of anger when goodness and truth and love have been violated. We should share in God's own anger at such things, in his "wrath" or "righteous indignation" (a better term might be something like "burning sorrow").

Jesus rebuked the Pharisees and scribes, and stormed angrily through the Temple because of what the Jewish establishment had become. Yet he prayed for their forgiveness when they engineered his death.

Forgiveness is not a feeling, it's a fact.

Jesus' own mother must have plumbed the depths of torment and grief when she stood watching her son's cruel death. Looking down from the cross, Jesus saw that Mary needed a strong and comforting arm around her, and probably a shoulder to cry on. So he asked John, his disciple, to look after her: "Woman, behold, your son!" "Behold, your mother!" (John 19:26-27).

I cannot believe that in Mary's anguish she vowed revenge against us, the entire human race, who crucified him. Grief can coexist with a willingness to forgive. It is right to allow ourselves to feel the hurt fully, and even to feel the *desire* to hit back. But the crucial question is whether we let these emotions become destructive forces in our behavior. God's grace can make it possible for us to find hidden supplies of generosity in ourselves, even as we experience the terrible battering of pain and grief.

* * *

As they crucified him, Jesus said, "Father, forgive them; for they know not what they do." Luke 23:34

ELEVEN

Healing and Childhood

Forgiving people who hurt us is easier when we picture them as little children.

THE LATE ANGLICAN BISHOP Leonard Wilson was tortured by the Japanese in Singapore during the Second World War. On some days he was hung upside-down in the blazing sun; he was also whipped while lying face-upwards on a table. He spoke afterwards about his experience.

I looked at their faces as they stood round and took it in turns to flog me, and their faces were hard and cruel, and some were evidently enjoying their cruelty. But by the grace of God I saw those men, not as they were, but as they had been. Once they were little children playing with their brothers and sisters, in those far-off days before they had been conditioned by their false nationalistic ideals; and it is hard to hate little children....

I knew it was only common sense to say "Forgive."[9]

Whenever people are rude or unkind to you, try imagining what they looked like as babies or toddlers. Somehow that takes the sting out of the situation and reduces everyone to an equal level.

I tried that once. But the picture which came to mind was

of a nasty, pampered little horror, screaming for its own way and getting it. "Well!" I thought, "so much for that exercise."

But then it struck me that the child I was imagining was behaving like that largely because his parents had spoiled him. I tried going back further and imagining him as a tiny baby. That helped a lot, and I realized how infinitely God loves that person.

* * *

They even brought babies for him to touch; but when the disciples saw them they scolded them for it. But Jesus called for the children and said, "Let the little ones come to me; do not try to stop them; for the kingdom of God belongs to such as these."

Luke 18:15-16, NEB

TWELVE

Old Hurts

Even if we have done our best to forgive, we will not necessarily stop hurting. We may have to pray through old hurts again and again over a long period of time.

People often feel guilty when harsh memories keep returning, as if there were something wrong with their efforts to forgive. But there is no need to feel that. Forgiving does not automatically mean forgetting. If it did, forgiveness would be easy and shallow, instead of the costly thing it really is.

M OST OF US CARRY AROUND a load of grievances and sore memories which are remarkably difficult to shed. Small things can remind us of something, and we start reliving the whole business all over again.

If pain from the past comes to mind, it is generally best to receive it head-on and let it flow through us. Pushing it away will only make the wound fester deep within us. Some people have benefited greatly from imagining Jesus standing beside or behind them when they remember painful scenes. Others do not find imaginative prayer helpful, and have to make do with just being there, in the middle of pain, however foolish that might feel, and letting that be their prayer.

We sometimes read about sudden transformations in

people's lives, stories about how they have opened up their past to Christ and asked for his healing to pour into them. Such transformations are wonderful, and we should praise God for them. But that kind of change doesn't happen for everyone, and it is a terrible distortion of Christian healing if people are made to feel guilty because they are still hurt by past wrongs, even after praying for inner healing. God works in each of us differently, and it may be that he wants us to work through the pain more slowly by facing it *with him.*

If we genuinely *want* to forgive, our basic desire still stands, no matter how many painful memories continue to shake us.

Sometimes, people continue to be damaged long after the initial deed. None of us can deal with past, present, and future in one attempt. As various repercussions hit us we have to face them one at a time. We are all in the middle of the process between the beginning of forgiveness and its ultimate fulfillment. As long as we keep offering our memories to God, guilt is the last thing we should feel when old wounds continue to take their toll.

* * *

Lord, this is what happened....
I give it all to you, every detail, every hurt, the big things
    and the petty things;
Let the pain I feel be for healing, and not a spring
    of bitterness.
Make my wound Christ-centered and for people, rather
    than self-centered and against them.

"Peace I leave with you; my peace I give to you; not as the world gives do I give to you. Let not your hearts be troubled, neither let them be afraid." John 14:27

THIRTEEN

Remember or Forget?

Forgetting is like sleep. You can never force it to happen. And the more you try to do it, the less likely you are to succeed.

To forget about past hurts is a gift, which is more likely to come if you have exposed the painful memories to God first.

A YOUNG MAN WHO HAD BEEN beaten up says he could not erase the memory from his mind. Instead he had to face it, and, by doing so, was able to help other people come to terms with their fears and loss of confidence.

On the other hand, a Jew who suffered terribly in a Nazi concentration camp says that he only found peace when he could forget what was done to him.

Which of them is right? Should we remember, or should we forget? Should we pray through old hurts or forget them?

I think the answer is *both*. Remembering and forgetting are things that happen to us, rather than things we should try to force ourselves to do.

When painful events from the past invade our prayers, it can do more harm than good to try to repress them. We may need to "run through the spool" of those experiences many times before the wounds begin to heal.

But after going through the story with God yet again, it is generally best to place the whole business in his hands, so that we are not totally dominated by it. It helps to have something specific to which we can turn our attention, like a Bible passage or something for meditation. Then the forgetfulness which heals is more likely to come.

In my own experience, I was only able to start forgetting some very deep hurts from the past when I poured out all the details to a wise and trusted priest in the confessional. It took about half an hour.

That night I woke in the early hours, with the words "It is redeemed" burning in my mind. (I'm not normally big on voices and visions, but this was very clear.) My eyes fell onto a cross on the wall of my bedroom, and I knew that Jesus had indeed dealt with the source of much past unhappiness and resulting depression. It was as if forgiveness and healing were pouring down from the cross into all those past events, in some way beyond my comprehension.

The old memories are still sparked off from time to time. But now it is not just a destructive pain; it is a redeemed pain, which I believe heals not only me, but also the people who hurt me.

It was prayer and sacrament together which enabled me to receive this gift of Christ's healing power in such a deep way. Other people will experience differently the same reality—that Christ is ultimately stronger than all evil.

* * *

Lord, delve deeply into my being,
and make me your dwelling-place,
Where all darkness is penetrated by your light,
all troubles calmed by your peace,
all evil redeemed by your love,
and all pain transformed in your suffering.

Based on a prayer by Jim Cotter[10]

FOURTEEN

When Someone Has Not Forgiven You

Much is said about the need to forgive others and let go of old resentments. But what if a person holds something against you, in such a way that you feel powerless to do anything about it?

God does not usually rally in spectacular fashion to "vindicate our cause" or "crush our foes beneath our feet." He seems to do the opposite, enabling us to find peace by leaving the other person free to forgive us or not, as he will. This is not weakness; it is strength, beyond our capacity alone, but possible with God when we stay close to him.

M ANY OF US FACE the unpleasant experience of not being forgiven at some point in our lives. People nurse a grudge against us over some mistake we have made or wrong we have done them, and nothing we do by way of apology seems to soften their resentment.

In some families, relatives refuse to talk to each other for years, and are only reconciled when one of them is on his death bed, if then. A surprising number of people live in a state of permanent bitterness.

Praying with the knowledge that we have not been forgiven is hard, because we easily slip into self-pity and begin to rehearse a string of arguments about how unreasonable people are. We do need to allow ourselves room to feel bad about what has happened, but then we have to shake ourselves free and widen our horizons.

Even Jesus was sometimes unforgiven, though unlike us he never sinned. His fellow townsfolk in Nazareth couldn't bear it when he stood up in their synagogue and proclaimed that he was fulfilling the hopes of the Old Testament; they were so furious that they tried to kill him (Luke 4:16-30). Many of the scribes and Pharisees found it impossible to forgive Jesus for seemingly undermining their sacred Law.

Quite likely, the families of some of the disciples also resented the demands that Jesus made. What did Peter's wife think about Jesus taking her husband away from his home and work? And what about Judas' family? Did they ever forgive Jesus for what happened to him (Matthew 27:3-5)?

Unlike Jesus, we do make mistakes and we sin against others. But it helps to remember that we are not alone in the painful experience of not being forgiven.

Sometimes we may wonder if the person with a grudge against us has some power over us. But that power is only there if we consent. God is our only judge. We are ultimately answerable only to God, not to any human being. God understands, accepts, and forgives us, and that is what matters. His mercy is like a fire which consumes and disintegrates the bitter wood of other people's resentment, which may have lodged itself inside us.

Consider, for a moment, the following fictional story. Two sisters in their fifties who live together find that they are increasingly getting on each other's nerves. The atmosphere at home is so bad that Sarah, the younger one, decides that she must have some time on her own. So she goes to stay with a friend.

Two weeks later, while Sarah is still away, her sister, Joyce, commits suicide. Sarah is devastated, and believes that she will never be free of the guilt she feels over her sister's death.

Sarah has to embark on the long, painful process of saying yes to this awful pain. Her anguish is not meant to destroy her; God has dealt with her sins, and she is forgiven. But she has to bear the pain for Joyce. It is as if Joyce handed over to Sarah a great burden of unhappiness, which she herself could not carry any longer in this life. If there was an element of spite in Joyce's action—to make Sarah feel guilty—the sting will be lessened if Sarah accepts the pain for Joyce's sake. Sarah's "yes" is a way of letting Joyce go; it helps Sarah to make something positive of Joyce's apparent refusal to forgive.

* * *

"Set your troubled hearts at rest, and banish your fears... Be assured, I am with you always, to the end of time" (John 14:27; Matthew 28:20, NEB).

"God said to me, 'I am mercy within mercy within mercy.'" [11]

FIFTEEN

Your Hurt Is Part of the Pain of the World

Our hurt is part of the pain of the world. We are not isolated units of human existence, each grinding along its lonely track. When one person is damaged, we are all affected, because of our shared humanity. Praying with our own pain can be a way of acknowledging this essential link between us and millions of others who are suffering in countless different ways. When we bring our troubles to God for the sake of the world as well as for ourselves, we become part of the "priesthood of all believers."

S OME TIME AGO I performed in a local concert. While waiting for my cue, I sat near the side of the stage, absorbed in my knitting. I was dimly aware of a few irritated glances, but didn't realize how much I was in the way until the producer came up and said, "Would you move, please? It's a nuisance having you sit there." The blood rushed to my cheeks as I searched for a quiet corner to nurse my wounded pride.

A trivial event, certainly. But for a moment I knew what it was like to be unwanted. I wondered what it would feel like to be rejected simply because of the color of your skin. What would it be like to be one of the thousands of homeless people living on the streets, subject to the glares of passing shoppers?

Because of the silly incident near the stage, I felt more motivated to pray for the forgotten people of the world. I had a tiny taste of their experience, and I could offer my hurt as a prayer for all the homeless and marginalised, whether in New York City or South Africa.

I realized with shame my own indifference to the fate of such people.

SOLIDARITY THROUGH WEAKNESS

Most of us feel helpless when confronted by the appalling problems of the world. We wonder if our feeble efforts at prayer and action are of any use at all.

We forget that our sense of weakness is itself something that we can offer to God. I began to realize this during my small involvement with the campaign to release several Russian Christians, including Irina Ratushinskaya, the poetess, and Alexander Ogorodnikov, who was imprisoned for holding Christian discussion groups in his apartment.

At times I felt deeply frustrated, because I feared those Christians might never know that we were caring and praying for them. "Why bother, then?" whispered the tempter.

But I have come to realize that this sense of helplessness is my common link with all prisoners of conscience and victims of disaster. None of us is the "strong one," dishing out our charity and prayers from a position of strength. Weakness is something we share with every human being, particularly those at the bottom of the totem pole. This shared suffering is the bond between us. If offered to Jesus, it generates an energy of love through our prayer.

Former Secretary of State, George Schultz, made a statement in 1987 concerning United States hostages in Lebanon.

"When an American is kicked around," he said, "we are all kicked around." I would prefer to say, "When anybody is kicked around, we're all kicked around."

We are all part of the blindness and selfishness of the world; we all wound others, even if our weapons are words rather than boots. So in prayer we can bring to God the sinfulness of the world, because we are very much a part of it.

"God chose what is foolish in the world to shame the wise, God chose what is weak in the world to shame the strong" (1 Corinthians 1:27).

We so often underestimate the power of the Holy Spirit working through prayer. Irina Ratushinskaya was held in freezing conditions, but was literally warmed by the prayers of ordinary people like us. She writes:

Believe me, it was often thus:
In solitary cells, on winter nights,
a sudden sense of joy and warmth
And a resounding note of love...
In the most fearful prison hour.[12]

* * *

Lord, let my sorrow and pain become part of your healing and redeeming of the world.

SIXTEEN

Energies Let Loose in the World

Chains of hurt are easy to identify. Less obvious, but just as real, are chains of healing. When we forgive, an energy of love and reconciliation is released into the world, which may have consequences far beyond our knowledge.

THE HURT AND PAIN we experience from others often results from a string of circumstances which have nothing directly to do with us.

For example, consider the experience of the elderly Miss Jones one morning at the dentist's office. When called from the waiting room she dropped her gloves onto the floor. Stiff and slow from the pain of arthritis, she stooped down carefully to pick them up. The hygienist, we'll call her Mrs. Sharp, snapped, "We haven't got all day, you know."

Miss Jones naturally felt hurt. But what she didn't know was that Mrs. Sharp's husband came home drunk and foul-mouthed last night.

Mr. Sharp had been drinking because he was depressed since becoming unemployed....

He had lost his job because a jealous coworker falsely accused him of a serious infraction of company policy.

One could go on and on, tracing factors that made one wrong lead to another. Miss Jones would have been surprised to realize that she was being touched by the universal human ills of unemployment, injustice, and resentment.

Much of our unhappiness is the product of a similar chain of hurt. Of course it would be absurd to analyze every trivial matter, as if to say, "My wife is nagging me because her mother forced her to eat lima beans when she was a child." But whenever we pray through a hurtful incident, it will help to consider what lies behind the event, and to remember that our reaction can have wide repercussions, contributing either to the hatred or to the healing of all human beings.

We are part of something far greater than we imagine. We affect other people all the time, simply by what we are. Any individual act of forgiving, however small, changes the world for the better. The archaic syndrome of "an eye for an eye" and "a life for a life" is only broken by Jesus' sort of loving, which allows God to transform pain into the miracle of forgiveness.

* * *

I touch and am touched by people.... Together, during the span of our lives, by loving or withholding love, we shall have created or destroyed something of humanity." **Prue Wilson**[13]

SEVENTEEN

You Are Going to Get Hurt

Anyone who takes his Christian commitment seriously will find that pain will be an integral part of his calling. This is not to say that pain should be sought for its own sake. Self-conscious "martyrs" don't do anyone any good. Yet it does seem that tension and conflict, far from being unhelpful in the Christian life, are actually fundamental to it.

The heart of God's redeeming work is the cross, the point where our evil and his love meet in unfathomable suffering. A good deal of prayer is about being there with God, right in the midst of the pain.

W HAT IS YOUR PARTICULAR AREA OF CHALLENGE? You may be the only Christian where you work. Perhaps fellow workers mock you about your faith. Or maybe you've worked hard on some international charity and have recently been accused of ignoring local charities. Or perhaps some people in your church show nothing but contempt for traditions of worship that have meant a great deal to you.

The list could go on forever.

When something bad happens to us, we hate it. We are upset, not just because of the hurt, but because we realize that important principles are under attack. This is a natural reaction, which Jesus himself expressed: "O faithless generation, how long am I to be with you? How long am I to bear with you?" (Mark 9:19).

But Jesus' way of looking at pain also helps us to cope with these hurtful tensions. "Blessed are you when men revile you and persecute you and utter all kinds of evil against you falsely on my account" (Matthew 5:11). "... In the world you have tribulation; but be of good cheer, I have overcome the world" (John 16:33).

Jesus' utter faithfulness to God brought inevitable conflict. As soon as he started preaching, he aroused hostility and opposition. His family thought he was mad, and tried to stop him from teaching (Mark 3:21). The scribes and Pharisees were filled with righteous indignation when he mixed with disreputable people and healed on the Sabbath. The hardliners in the establishment started wishing him dead as soon as he began to make people alive.

Betrayed, denied, and abandoned by his disciples, Jesus trod a path of humiliation in the eyes of the world. And he invites us to join him on the same path: "Anyone who wishes to be a follower of mine must leave self behind; he must take up his cross and come with me" (Mark 8:34, NEB).

We cannot avoid conflict with those who exploit others or who greedily abuse the natural world. We are bound to be distressed by people's hard and unforgiving attitudes, by apathy outside the church and judgmentalism within it. If anything, prayer makes us more aware rather than less aware of what is going on around us. We become involved in the suffering of others, absorbing with Christ some of the barbs and blows with which human beings wound each other. To hunger and thirst for righteousness and peace may be blessed, but it is also extremely costly.

We do not stand sinless in the middle of a world of sinners. But, as salt in a stew or leaven in a loaf of bread, we do have a very special and demanding role as Christians among the people with whom we live.

We know this in theory. Most of us think we are ready to take up our cross and follow Christ. Yet, when the suffering comes, it feels neither heroic nor glamorous, and we do our best to escape it. Pain is unpleasant, and we heartily wish that God would do something to rid us of it as soon as possible. But the only alternative is a safe cocoon of ignorance and loneliness. Saving our own life would be much easier; but at what cost? "For whoever would save his life will lose it; and whoever loses his life for my sake and the gospel's will save it" (Mark 8:35).

Not long ago I attended a prayer meeting for South Africa. Someone read aloud a report detailing the circumstances in which a black teenage boy had been reduced to a vegetable after beatings and electric shocks from security police. In the time of prayer that followed, the frustrated young man sitting next to me prayed, "Oh God, I feel so angry. I want revenge on the people who do these things. God, forgive me."

And he wept.

The misery and shame we feel when we desire revenge can sometimes be a part of the suffering placed upon us. We are part of the pain and evil of the world, and are shaken both by the loftiest and the basest motives. Only by offering all this to God in prayer can it be redeemed, from the inside.

TWO PARABLES OF DISCIPLESHIP

A friend of mine attended a party recently in which one of the other guests loudly remarked: "I'm not a racist, but I can't bear all those black faces in line at the checkout counter every day." My friend felt the blood rising to his cheeks, and plunged into a heated argument. Some people at the party were maddeningly flippant, while others were blatantly prejudiced. In his embarrassment, the host teased my friend, saying, "You Christians are such goody-goodies."

My friend left the party feeling as though he had made a mess of the whole business. He wished he could have expressed certain points more convincingly.

Frustration of this sort is the cost of caring, and the cost of discipleship. Simply offering God the pain of such encounters is creative, even if there are no apparent "results."

Another story, from the Philippines, tells about a fine bamboo tree which grew on a large estate. One day the owner came to cut it down. The bamboo begged to be spared, but to no avail. "You are needed for a water pipe," he was told, "because there has been a drought."

So the bamboo agreed; but worse was to come. Each partition inside the joints in his huge, hollow stem had to be cut out. Again he protested. But when he saw the parched fields and half-starved families, he relented.

After he had been carved out as a channel of life-giving water for all those people, he was glad that he no longer stood secure and untouched in the plantation.

* * *

...*"The very stone which the builders rejected has become the head of the corner."* Mark 12:10

Lord Jesus, it is when you are most unwanted, kicked around, and useless in worldly terms, that you are most acutely and keenly present.

EIGHTEEN

Watch Out!

When we learn to suffer a little, the devil has a curious knack of creeping in. It can begin subtly enough. We may start congratulating ourselves for suffering more than other people, or we may even conclude that God thinks we are more virtuous than most.

This kind of self-focus only narrows our vision, clogs up the channels of God's mercy and grace, and detracts from anything we may have done for Christ anyway.

W HO HASN'T KNOWN SOMEONE who will never let us forget how much he has endured in a good cause? Sometimes such people think they can lay down the law for everyone else, as though their trials have given them some sort of unique contact with the Holy Spirit. Or, they may expect permanent sympathy and endless concessions from everybody. If we're not careful, this same attitude will start showing up in our hearts too. We may find ourselves saying, "But, I've been working so hard...."

Jesus gave short shrift to such attitudes in his parable about the hardworking slave (Luke 17:7-10, NEB).

Suppose one of you has a servant ploughing or minding sheep. When he comes back from the fields, will the master say, "Come along at once and sit down"? Will he not rather say, "Prepare my supper, fasten your belt, and then wait on me while I have my meal; you can have yours afterwards"? Is he grateful to the servant for carrying out his orders? So with you: When you have carried out all your orders, you should say, "We are servants and deserve no credit; we have only done our duty."

* * *

A good way to pray when we slip into self-satisfaction is to share our silliness with God, and picture ourselves standing on the pedestal that we seem to want, labeled: SPECIAL CASE, THE CENTER OF THE UNIVERSE.

NINETEEN

Weeping As Prayer

*Frustration and misery about human suffering can some-
times drive us to tears; we feel so useless and without hope
of a solution. But the weeping can itself be offered as
prayer.*

A FRIEND ONCE TOLD ME how she had been deeply distressed about a famine in Africa, and had wanted to do
all she could to respond to the need. At a meeting of her
church council she had tried to raise the issue, but everyone
was so preoccupied with organizing a church supper that
there wasn't time. What angered her most was that a great
deal of energy had been thrown into arguments about table
decorations. People were dying of hunger while the debate
raged over flower arrangements.

She went home and wept in sheer frustration. The next
day she sat down to pray, but wondered how she could do
so when she felt so depressed and frustrated. But her pain
and anger were her prayer at that moment for the starving
people of the world. Her weeping was as important a part of
her offering as her subsequent charitable actions.

Two other friends have told me how they wept over news
items. One of them cried and prayed while the Zeebrugge
ferry disaster was going on in 1987, and felt that God was
drawing her to be deeply involved in the suffering of others.

65

Another friend found himself weeping at the murder of a whole family in Khartoum, whose children were the same age as his; again, he identified emotionally with them.

Clare Amos provides another graphic example of how weeping can be intercession for those in great suffering. I quote at length:

> I was revisiting St. George's Cathedral—the focal point of the Anglican Diocese of Jerusalem—where once I used to work.... A group of us Westerners wanted to visit a Palestinian refugee camp. Jazalone was chosen, about ten to fifteen miles from Jerusalem....
>
> One of the party asked if we could see a refugee home. After some hesitation we were taken to visit a home which contained a woman with three small children around her. It was one room, no bigger than the average English lounge.... We asked how many people lived there. Fourteen. All in this one room? "Well," said the woman of the house, "we used to have three rooms. But the Israelis came and concreted over the entrance to the other two so that we can't use them."
>
> The woman told us why. Her oldest son had been deported after he had finished a jail sentence for anti-Israeli activities. Her second son was currently in prison. The third boy was due to be sentenced....
>
> After the woman had finished telling us all this, one of her three toddlers piped up—a boy of about five—"And when I grow up I'm going to go to prison too."
>
> ... That child's thoughtless remark seemed the most terrible thing of all. For he is perhaps right. Perhaps the hopelessness is the special horror of the Middle East, and of the conflict between Palestinians and Israelis. There is one land, and there are two peoples, both with a history of suffering, and who both claim it....
>
> Is that boy also destined to become enmeshed in the cycle of violence—his powerless grey-black future compen-

sated for only by the bitterness of his anger? And that woman, his mother, what must be her thoughts as she raises her children as fodder for Israeli jails? Hers is surely a hopelessness that few of us in England can begin to fathom....

We returned to Jerusalem, to the slightly faded but still secure bastion of St. George's. And I wept, wept from a sense of frustration laced with guilt. Guilt for having a comfortable home in Cambridge, guilt for the mess the British mandate had created in Palestine, frustration because I felt powerless and could do nothing....

And then I realized that perhaps in weeping I am in fact doing something important. Weeping expresses my common humanity with Arab and Israeli that transcends our divisions. Somehow when we weep we express the fact that we can't control our world, or indeed our human existence, or life or death. We acknowledge our dependence and our powerlessness, but beyond that, our love....

"See how he must have loved him," they said of Jesus as they watched him weeping for his dead friend, Lazarus. Weeping and love belong together. For the world's ultimate sanity men as well as women will have to learn how to weep....

And, in some mysterious way, tears can begin to lead to resurrection, they are agents of transformation. Only those that sow in tears are told that they shall reap in joy. We are promised that there will come a time when God will wipe away all tears from our eyes. But that is a promise even God cannot keep unless we first learn how to weep.[14]

* * *

When you weep,
You have a unique opportunity
To give this dark thing to God—
An offering from the inside of the shadow.

It is as if you bring the whole world with you.
This is the priesthood of all believers:
Christians in the mud with the rest,
Reaching out to God on behalf of us all;
And sharing the pain of creation with its Creator.

Part Two

Praying with Your Sinfulness

It is said that St. Jerome, the great fourth-century biblical scholar, once said to Jesus in a dream, "Lord, what can I give to you? My money? My books? Or my learning?"

And the Lord replied, "Give me your sins; give me your desires."

TWENTY

Into the Sun and Wind of God

What are we to do with our selfishness and sin? It rarely works to make grand resolutions, telling ourselves that we will never again fall into familiar errors. We need instead to turn away from self-preoccupation, and focus our attention on God, so that he can do the transforming work in us that we cannot do on our own.

PEOPLE HAVE ALL SORTS of popular misconceptions about the prayer of repentance. Some think that we can only come to God full of guilt and dread, because he seems such a judgmental figure. Others suppose that repentance is basically an academic exercise, consisting of a thorough check of all conceivable ways we may have broken the Ten Commandments. We are to rack our brains in order to try to remember when the infraction occurred.

In churches which practice the sacrament of penance, a popular caricature is of the person who sins as much as he likes on Friday night, because he knows the priest will absolve him on Saturday morning. This makes penitential prayer nothing more than a sham.

We need another picture.

71

A PARABLE AT SEA

I once observed a family on the cross-channel ferry from Folkstone, England, to Boulogne, France. They were obviously on a day trip, and our ship would soon be setting sail.

Half an hour passed, and we still hadn't moved; one hour, and by then the children were restless and crabby. Their mother was feeling harassed and was trying vainly to amuse them, becoming increasingly irritable every time they asked, "When are we going?"

Dad went off to the lounge in disgust.

Eventually we left Folkstone. A short while later dad came back, beer in hand, complaining, "Now we'll only have a short time in France before we have to go back again."

The children then began to argue over who should read which comic book. Eventually their mother declared, "Okay. We're not going to have any more arguments today!" Everyone sank into a gloomy silence.

But gradually the scene was transformed. The sheer exhilaration of the sun and wind, the colors of the sea, and the distant view of Dover's cliffs, combined to lift everyone out of a bad mood into something infinitely greater.

The children were the first to be affected. They stood at the rail, soaking up the sunshine and the smells and the sound of the sea. Then mom put down her newspaper, and she began to laugh with the children about the sea gulls perched in comical places on the mast. In the end, dad went and joined them as well.

It was as if the irritation and whining had been absorbed and dissolved in the refreshing breeze and movement of the sea voyage. The family had found itself again, not because they had sat down and had a long discussion about how to get along together, but because they had been swept up into something bigger than themselves. They had turned around, stood next to each other, and let themselves be drawn into the sunshine. I cannot count how many times I have said to myself, "I will never be irritable again," or, "I will not make any more thoughtless remarks." But it never works, and sooner or later I slip into the same old pitfalls once more. My mistake in these resolutions is to assume that I can overcome my sinfulness simply by my own efforts. I am forgetting that the most important factor enabling me to resist sin is God's wonderful grace.

Once we have realized and confessed our sins, it is best to turn away from ourselves and, instead, turn to God, like the family on the ship turning their faces into the wind and sun. Then our love of God and desire to do his will can swallow up our petty selfishness, so that it begins to loosen its hold on us.

Concentrating on self-improvement only leads to despair.

Concentrating on God makes forgiveness and transformation possible.

Later on we may notice, with surprise, that changes are taking place in us after all.

* * *

"Behold, I am doing a new thing;
  now it springs forth, do you not perceive it?...
I, I am He
  who blots out your transgressions for my own sake,
  and I will not remember your sins.
I have swept away your transgressions like a cloud,
  and your sins like mist;
return to me, for I have redeemed you." Isaiah 43:19, 25; 44:22

  Let me open my eyes to the glory and the sunshine of God in his creation.
  Let me open my heart to receive the full impact of his love.

Let his radiant fire burn away all that is rotten in me.

Let me breathe in the fresh air of life, on which I depend in the miracle of existence.

Let the wind of God's Spirit blow through me and clear away the cobwebs and the garbage.

I surrender my whole being to the wind and sun of God's love.

"And we all, with unveiled face, beholding the glory of the Lord, are being changed into his likeness from one degree of glory to another..." (2 Corinthians 3:18).

TWENTY-ONE

What, No Struggle?

Just because grandiose resolutions to overcome our sins are seldom successful does not mean that we are excused from the fight against evil. We all have to struggle against a whole range of temptations and selfish impulses.

"Repenting" means literally "turning around," away from self and toward God, for forgiveness and strength. This is where the main battle lies, because the pull of evil can be unnervingly strong.

HOW DO YOU PRAY when you feel tempted to have an affair, or when you feel like getting revenge on someone? Prayer seems almost impossible when such destructive emotions are at their highest.

If we try to repress our desires, we only become their slaves. A strong emotion is a fact which must be faced, however unpalatable; what matters is what we do with it. We have to open up our selfish inclinations to Christ, again and again if necessary, so that he can purge and purify them.

Wallowing in self-contempt is unhealthy, because it focuses our attention on ourselves. We do better to make a beeline for Jesus, and concentrate on the way he lived and taught. It is being with him that changes us. Jesus had a party with the tax gatherers and ruffians of Capernaum before they began to examine their consciences!

And Levi made him a great feast in his house; and there was a large company of tax collectors and others sitting at table with them. And the Pharisees and their scribes murmured against his disciples, saying, "Why do you eat and drink with tax collectors and sinners?" And Jesus answered them, "Those who are well have no need of a physician, but those who are sick; I have not come to call the righteous, but sinners to repentance." **Luke 5:29-32**

If we see a characteristic weakness repeated in ourselves it helps to use a specific phrase or prayer with which to confront it. For example, perhaps my weakness consists of a desire to avoid conflict no matter what; this temptation has to be met, not just by telling myself to be bolder, but with another weapon: the words of Jesus. I can repeat his words to myself: "In the world you have tribulation; but be of good cheer, I have overcome the world" (John 16:33). Or when I wish I could be less irritable, I can use a prayer like "Jesus, live in me," rather than simply nagging myself about keeping my mouth shut. The work of overcoming sin is accomplished through partnership with God, not through a solo struggle.

Of course, we need to be aware of our faults and of the effect our selfishness has on other people. But without the additional help of something greater than our own willpower, we will not get very far.

* * *

"...we have believed in Christ Jesus, in order to be justified by faith in Christ, and not by works of the law, because by works of the law shall no one be justified" (Galatians 2:16).

A person who wishes to begin a good life should be like a man who draws a circle. Let him get the center in the right place and keep it so and the circumference will be good. In other words, let a man first learn to fix his heart on God, and then his good deeds will have virtue; but if a man's heart is unsteady even the great things he does will be of small advantage.   **Meister Johannes Eckhart 1260-1327**

Am I centered, rooted, and grounded in God? Everything I am and do springs from my center. I will never overcome self just by cutting away its fruits; the roots need to be dealt with, by being plunged deeply into God.

TWENTY-TWO

Guilt—Friend or Foe?

Guilt is meant to be a servant, not a master. Many people carry around a burden of unresolved guilt, which becomes a significant block to prayer, destroys self-respect, and takes away inward peace.

If it is functioning properly, however, guilt eventually puts itself out of a job.

G UILT PLAYS AN IMPORTANT ROLE in our lives. Being Christian does not provide us with an excuse to brush off our sins as if they did not matter.

But guilt is also liable to become exaggerated and distorted. If we are troubled by something we have done wrong, guilt can find a foothold inside us, until we begin to imagine that we are beyond redemption. However many times we confess our sins to God, we never really feel that we are forgiven.

Destructive guilt needs to be turned on its head and transformed into the positive tool it was meant to be.

The very fact that we feel guilty is worth pondering. Why do we feel that way? Our shame must spring from a deep desire to live honestly and lovingly and to be reconciled with ourselves, other people, and God. Otherwise we would never have felt guilty in the first place.

Our desire for what is good and right is like a tiny flame, placed in us by God. We feel guilty because we know we

79

have betrayed that flame. But guilt should also lead us to God's forgiveness so that we can be freed from our burden.

How vividly I remember my first biology lesson in high school. I was rudely introduced to basic anatomy via a dissected rat. I felt strangely shocked at the way this small creature was totally opened up and exposed to us; nothing inside him was hidden from our gaze.

Some people who shoulder a burden of guilt think that prayer is going to be like that. They think that God is pointing an accusing finger at them and fear some awful exposure or humiliation if they approach him in prayer.

Nothing could be further from the truth. The gospel invites us to repent, yes. But repentance involves freedom and release. The primary message of Jesus, and the apostles after him, was simply: "Your sins are forgiven." The joyful, overwhelming, and illogical fact of being totally forgiven is the gospel!

The only similarity between Christian prayer and the fate of the unfortunate rat is that there is no way we can hide our inner darkness from God. But there still remains a huge difference. When we allow God to open us up, we are not brutally dismembered or surrounded by curious, mocking stares. The only eyes gazing on us are the compassionate and gentle eyes of Christ. We will, of course, feel sad and ashamed when our sinfulness is laid bare before him. But we have nothing to fear.

We can never earn our salvation by our own efforts. Forgiveness is God's free gift, the outrageous miracle of undeserved mercy which he is waiting to offer us, if we will only turn in faith and receive it. But if we refuse to open up, parts of us will remain cold and unhealed.

* * *

If you are feeling the pain of guilt, it is worth making space for a time of solitude with God (even if you can only find five or ten minutes), so that you can open it all up to him.

Expose your memories before God, without fear. Tell him everything and let him know how sorry you are. He is waiting to stretch out his arms to you.

Turn your face toward him in complete confidence. Allow his mercy and love to soak deeply into you.

Forget about the details of what you did wrong. Concentrate instead on the God who loves you.

Hear him say to you: "I have relieved your shoulder of the burden... In distress you called, and I delivered you..."

Psalm 81:6-7

You are my beloved child; my heart yearns for you, and I will surely have mercy on you. Jeremiah 31:20

"Your sins are forgiven...." Mark 2:5

Music can feature in this sort of prayer. There is a lovely melody by Gretry, the *Air de Ballet*, from the opera *Zemire et Azor*[1]. The plot is based on the fairy tale *Beauty and the Beast*, and this section of the opera conveys the pure love of Beauty, which has the power to restore the Beast to his real self. So this music is particularly appropriate when we are asking God to love and transform the beast in us into the person we were meant to be. It is especially helpful to read verses from the Bible (such as those quoted above) immediately before listening, or while the music is playing.

Many other pieces of music can enhance prayer in this way. Possibilities include:[2]

Bach: Double Violin Concerto, 2nd movement.

Bach: Concerto for Oboe and Strings, BWV 1 060, 2nd movement.

Beethoven: Piano Concerto No. 5 (Emperor), 2nd movement.

TWENTY-THREE

The Stab of Remorse

Some of the most poignant scenes in any drama occur when a miserable person is gently encouraged to turn his face toward a compassionate person. Praying with our sins is like that. God is not there to make us feel wretched; nor is he keeping us at arm's length. He is intimately close, waiting for us to turn and receive his forgiveness.

WHAT A HORRIBLE SENSATION it is to realize that you have hurt someone, especially if you love that person. A flash of irritation, a thoughtless remark, or a sharp reprimand can bring on a sharp stab of remorse afterward. Even when you apologize, the other person still feels the hurt, and you wish you could do more to put things right.

We can, in fact, do something constructive with the pain of remorse. We can face it and bear it as a prayer for the people we have hurt.

The desire to put things right by doing something specific is a natural instinct. On more than one occasion I have brought home a small gift for my husband after we have had an argument. It helps to have a tangible object as an outward sign of our desire to make amends.

But when it comes to putting things right between us and God, we cannot. The debt we owe him is so great, we can never "make it up," even in a dozen lifetimes. Much of the elaborate Old Testament sacrificial system expressed this fundamental longing to set things right between us and God. But the startling news that Jesus brought is that God does not require this of us. Like the father of the prodigal son, God simply waits to approach and embrace us when we turn back to him.

The son in that parable badly wanted to prove how sorry he was. He had it all worked out, and had planned to say to his father: "I am no longer worthy to be called your son; treat me as one of your hired servants."

But all he got for his pains was an enormous hug. Before he had a chance to finish his speech, his delighted father instructed the servants: "Bring quickly the best robe, and put it on him; and put a ring on his hand, and shoes on his feet... let us eat and make merry" (Luke 15:18-25).

Jesus' sacrifice on the cross was the incredible final solution for the problem of our separation from God. He absorbed our human sinfulness in an act of total self-abandonment, and transformed it into the marvelous energy of resurrection madness, which swept through the first-century apostles. (At least it looked like madness to the rest of the world.) Jesus has saved us from the destructive power of guilt, as well as from the frightening dead-end of relying on ourselves alone.

The cross is beyond time. There is no evil that Jesus has not entered into; no gap between us and God that he has not bridged; and no wrong that he has not received into himself and overcome.

If Jesus has done all this for us, what is required on our part? Only that we should turn toward him in complete honesty, as we face the painful knowledge of our persistent betrayal of what we know to be right.

One of the most crucial verses in the Old Testament comes in Isaiah 30:15: "In returning [lit. turning] and rest you shall be saved; / in quietness and in trust shall be your strength."

Turn... return... turn again... in quietness and stillness—

this is Jesus' invitation, too, in the lifelong process of conversion.

The miracle of salvation is that we can say yes to God, even when we still have so much self-centeredness, greed and unkindness in our nature. He doesn't rub our noses in the mud, but instead offers us his unconditional forgiveness.

* * *

Love bade me welcome: yet my soul drew back,
  Guilty of dust and sin,
But quick-ey'd Love, observing me grow slack
  From my first entrance in,
Drew nearer to me, sweetly questioning,
  If I lack'd any thing.

A guest, I answer'd, worthy to be here:
  Love said, you shall be he.
I the unkind, ungrateful? Ah my dear,
  I cannot look on thee.
Love took my hand, and smiling did reply.
  Who made the eyes but I?

Truth Lord, but I have marr'd them: let my shame
  Go where it doth deserve.
And know you not, says Love, who bore the blame!
  My dear, then I will serve.
You must sit down, says Love, and taste my meat:
  So I did sit and eat. **George Herbert (1593-1633)** [3]

Jesus was left alone with the woman taken in adultery. "Jesus looked up and said to her, 'Woman, where are they? Has no one condemned you?' She said, 'No one, Lord.' And Jesus said, 'Neither do I condemn you; go, and do not sin again'" (John 8:10-11).

TWENTY-FOUR

Self-Protection

Self-protection underlies much of our sinfulness. When we are busy shielding ourselves, we slip all too easily into dishonesty and disloyalty; or else we build up defensive barriers which make us behave unkindly to other people.

At the painful moment when we realize that we have let God and our friends down, we cannot escape the consequences. We long for relief, but the truth has to be faced. The very fact that we feel wretched is a sign of hope because it shows that we do want to be true and compassionate people, deep down.

In prayer Jesus draws out of us this desire to love.

P ETER KNEW ALL ABOUT SELF-PROTECTION. What else but this caused him to deny his Master? Jesus had been arrested and dragged from one interrogation to another all night long. The terrified disciples had fled, and Peter was now restlessly hanging around in the courtyard of the high priest's house.

A servant-girl stared hard and challenged him: "You're one of that man's followers, aren't you!"

In a moment of sheer panic, Peter, who had loved Jesus so long and so faithfully, blurted out, "What on earth are you talking about? I tell you I don't know him."

Three times Peter denied all knowledge of Jesus. And then the cock crowed, and Peter rushed out and wept bitterly (Mark 14:53-72).

Most of us would have done the same.

We already do, in our own way. We are quick to make excuses for ourselves, often at the expense of others. And we don't mind hearing criticisms about people, because we are relieved to find a scapegoat, even when we know that the remarks being made are unjust.

How can we prevent this selfishness from spoiling our better nature? I am not sure that we can, on our own. But the way Jesus handled Peter gives us a clue to the way he deals with us when we are trying to protect ourselves.

DO YOU LOVE ME?

During the days immediately after the crucifixion, Peter must have carried an intolerable burden of guilt. He must have longed to show Jesus how desperately he regretted his cowardice. But there seemed to be no way of putting things right. Restless and miserable, he thought he might find relief by doing something practical. So he went fishing with a few other disciples on the Sea of Galilee.

The story is a familiar one (John 21). They caught nothing all night. Then they saw the figure of Jesus standing on the shore, and he suggested that they cast their net on the other side of the boat. The haul of fish was enormous.

Peter suddenly recognized Jesus, and leapt joyfully into the water, swimming to the shore.

And then, when the two men were face-to-face once more, it was Jesus who took the initiative to heal the guilt which was devouring Peter.

Peter had denied Jesus three times. So three times Jesus asked him, "Do you love me?"

Gradually Peter was able to see the real truth about himself. Beneath his surface desire to protect himself, he did indeed want to love and serve Christ.

Jesus had not said, "Peter, are you ever going to deny me again?" Instead he had asked the fundamental question: "Do you love me? What is your highest and best desire? Which way are you pulling—with me or against me?"

This is how Jesus will handle us, if we will let him. Our hope does not lie primarily in our own determination to mend our ways, but in our response to his simple question: "Do you love me?"

* * *

"As the life of Christ takes hold on us, our lives will be transformed from being lives of self-protection, self-care, self-cultivation, into lives given for others, because God, the God of compassion, will have taken possession of our being..." **Gerard Hughes** [4]

TWENTY-FIVE

Jealousy

O, beware, my lord, of jealousy;
It is the green-eyed monster which doth mock
The meat it feeds on.[5]

"I'M NOT A JEALOUS PERSON," we like to say to ourselves. That is probably true, inasmuch as we do not begrudge movie stars their fame or professors their brains. But we all have within us seeds of jealousy which occasionally rise to the surface.

We can feel threatened by a person whose work is similar to ours, who is attractive, about our age, and who is apparently more successful than we are. We don't like it when a colleague gets a job we had hoped for, and we are jealous of people who seem to be more popular, or receive more invitations to parties than we do.

It is a rare individual who will not wince inwardly when adverse comparisons are made:

"Mom, I wish you made cookies like Mrs. Johnson!" says one of the children, amid a chorus of agreement from the rest of the family.

"This guy has got to be the best quarterback we've had in the last twenty years," says a fan, in the hearing of last year's quarterback.

To our shame, most of us feel better when negative things

are said about the person we envy. Both the mother and the football player would probably be glad if someone else were to pipe up, "I don't agree! Mrs. Johnson's cookies are horrible!" or, "Maybe, but the new guy is not as experienced as he should be."

I have tried various ways of praying through my feelings about somebody I envy. I know in my heart of hearts that I wish the person no harm. So when I pray, I ask God to enable my better and deeper desire—for this person's good— to rise to the surface and swallow up my petty selfishness.

One exercise I have found helpful is to ask myself what would happen if I heard that a woman I envy had been badly injured in an automobile accident, or if something slanderous had been written about her in a newspaper. Then I picture myself visiting her. I know that my concern at that moment would override any jealousy I might have felt. Such thoughts are rather gruesome, but I find that they can help me to pray for certain people in a more genuine and caring way.

My children once had a book about a monster who terrorized a family. Finally, a little boy drew a pencil picture of it and then rubbed it out. Exit monster!

Jealousy is like an ugly monster which blunders around inside us, trampling on our desire for other people to blossom, and spewing out purple smoke which forms the word "self" in the air.

It can be fun and helpful to draw a picture of our own Jealousy Monster when praying. But what about rubbing it out? It's not as easy to get rid of jealousy as it is to erase a pencil-sketch.

The best way to deal with our feelings is to pray for the person we envy, faithfully and regularly. We cannot genuinely intercede for someone and simply dismiss him or her at the same time. Eventually we may find that the monster has vanished. Or perhaps it has turned into something else.

* * *

But who can discern his errors?
  Clear thou me from hidden faults. Psalm 19:12

Purge me with hyssop, and I shall be clean;
  wash me, and I shall be whiter than snow....
Create in me a clean heart, O God,
  and put a new and right spirit within me. Psalm 51:7, 10

TWENTY-SIX

What Do I Want?

Each of us is full of conflicting desires. We want to be generous, but we can be greedy and extravagant; we want to care about others, yet we put our own concerns first; we agree that we should stand up for what is right, yet we slip into compromises to make life easier for ourselves; we would hope to be peacemakers, yet we easily hurt people back.

Fortunately the matter does not end there. Our ungainly collection of desires is not a fixed or unchangeable part of our nature. Prayer gives God an opening, so that, through his work in us, our highest and best desires can have a bit more say in the way we live.

I WAS WATCHING MY SMALL SON one day in November. It was the last day of the month, and on the wall before him was an unopened Advent calendar, sparkling with glitter, every door a tantalizing mystery.

His small hand reached up and touched a window above the stable and felt its edges. Yet something held him back from opening it. Though longing to peep at the picture beneath, he also wanted to save the delight for the right day. He knew from experience that you spoil your own fun by cheating with an Advent calendar.

So he decided to wait. Conflicting desires had been pulling him in opposite directions, but the deeper urge, to save the excitement for the proper moment, had prevailed. He had stopped and given himself a chance to think about what mattered most.

Phyllis Bottome once wrote, "You are not free until your long desires are stronger than your short ones."[6] I find this a most penetrating remark. The term "short desires" suggest the things which clamor under our noses, to be quickly taken up in a selfish impulse; but a "long desire" conveys something more thoughtful, linked with ideals which have touched us at spiritual high points in our lives.

Our daydreams teach us a lot about our "short desires," because they whisk us into all sorts of adventures in which we usually play a flattering role, often at the expense of other people. It is alarming how easily our integrity can be suspended in these daydreams, before we realize what we are doing.

Involuntary fantasies reveal many things which need to be laid open to God and purified. But how can we enable this to take place?

RECOGNIZING OUR DESIRES

It is important to tell God exactly what we want, *not what we think we ought to want*. Nothing blocks the channels of communion with God more efficiently than pious self-deception. If we are honest, he can do something with us. Having put our selfish desires into words, it is useful to take them to their logical conclusion. Suppose we do want possessions, or power, or somebody else's spouse. What would happen if God always let us have our own way? Who would get hurt? What would we want next? What sort of person would we become?

What matters most to us?

BURIED TREASURE

Jesus said, "The kingdom of heaven is like treasure hidden in a field, which a man found and covered up; then in his joy he goes and sells all that he has, and buys that field" (Matthew 13:44). We do have grounds for hope that our better and deeper desires will prevail over our superficial ones, not because we are so virtuous, but because God is at work in us.

If we ask ourselves, "What do I want to be the most important thing in my life?" it may be that, in the end, we would say, "The love of God." If so, that is a discovery of buried treasure which was put in us by God in the first place. We can confidently trust him to nurture and rekindle this desire for his love, when we ask that our "shorter" desires may be taken over and absorbed by our "longer ones."

* * *

"You know better than I how much I love you, Lord. You know it and I know it not, for nothing is more hidden from me than the depths of my own heart.

I desire to love you; I fear that I do not love you enough.

I beseech you to grant me the fulness of pure love.

Behold my desire; you have given it to me. Behold in your creature what you have placed there. O God, you love me enough to inspire me to love you for ever; behold not my sins. Behold your mercy and my love." François Fenélon (1651-1715)

Lord, save me from being divided against myself. Let my will, inch by inch, become more completely yours.

TWENTY-SEVEN

Praying with Ambition

Ambitious thoughts can slither craftily into our stream of consciousness, revealing all sorts of hidden longings to exalt our own ego. Translating our selfish desires literally into prayer helps to put them in a different perspective.

O F ITSELF, AMBITION IS NOT WRONG. There is nothing to be ashamed of in hoping for a promotion or wanting to do great things. The ambition which harms is the sort which inflates one's self-esteem out of all proportion...

"If I were chosen for this position of honor, awarded such and such a prize, recognized as the best, noticed by important people..."

Thus our ego rattles on. We would be terribly embarrassed if our idle thoughts were suddenly made audible to the outside world.

Selfish ambition also distorts the way we see other people. We start thinking of them either as useful cogs or obstacles to our self-centered plans, rather than as fellow human beings.

There is little point in declaring that we will never indulge in such thoughts again; we know ourselves too well. Nor can most of us honestly pray, "Lord, please put me at the bottom of every pile, to be neglected and trodden on by all."

An indirect attack on selfish ambition is much more effective. Try laughing at yourself with a prayer like this: "Dear Lord, I want to be elected to the top committee, and I trust you will make everyone notice my skills. Keep all other candidates out of the limelight, O God, and silence those who know about my weaknesses, so that everyone will acknowledge my superiority and vote accordingly. Amen."

Such a travesty of true prayer helps us to laugh with God about ourselves, and cuts our ambition down to size. Maybe we can then move on to pray wholeheartedly, "Lord, I depend on you for my very existence, my skills, my experience, everything. And yet I want prestige and power for myself. Show me what really matters, and let my longer and better desires overtake my short ones!"

Being tempted by ambitious thoughts is not the same as behaving ambitiously. It is encouraging to remember that even Jesus was tempted by thoughts of ambition, when Satan offered him "all the kingdoms of the world and the glory of them" (Matthew 4:8). But Jesus chose the way of humiliation instead of the path of glory.

The crucified figure is not there to bully us into self-loathing. Love, not retribution, pours down from the cross. Yet, it is good for us to ponder the depth of suffering and degradation which Jesus endured for our sake, especially when our own ambitions are riding high.

* * *

When I survey the wondrous cross,
On which the Prince of glory died,
My richest gain I count but loss,
And pour contempt on all my pride. Isaac Watts (1674-1748)

"Have this mind among yourselves, which is yours in Christ Jesus, who, though he was in the form of God, did not count equality with God a thing to be grasped, but emptied himself, taking the form of a servant,... he humbled himself and became obedient unto death, even death on a cross" (Philippians 2:5-8).

TWENTY-EIGHT

The Path of Pride

Pride is one big hoax. It is plausible, because there is usually some truth in the evidence on which we congratulate ourselves, and it is dangerous, because we fail to see it. Lust you can't miss; anger you cannot avoid. But pride disguises itself as "moral superiority" or "spiritual maturity," so that before very long we have put on the Pharisee's distorting spectacles and thanked God that we are not like everyone else. **Luke 18:11**

PRIDE IS A CUNNING ANIMAL. It takes half the truth about ourselves and makes it look like the whole truth.

"You have a lot of boots," James murmured.

"I have a lot of legs," the Centipede answered proudly, "and a lot of feet. One hundred, to be exact."

"*There* he goes again!" the Earthworm cried, speaking for the first time. "He simply cannot stop telling lies about his legs! He doesn't have anything like a hundred of them! He's only got forty-two! The trouble is that most people don't bother to count them. They just take his word. And anyway, there is nothing *marvellous*, you know, Centipede, about having a lot of legs."

"Poor fellow," the Centipede said, whispering in

James's ear. "He's blind. He can't see how splendid I look."

"In my opinion," the Earthworm said, "the *really* marvelous thing is to have no legs at all, and to be able to walk just the same."

"You call that *walking*!" cried the Centipede.

"You're a *slitherer*, that's all you are!" [7]

Pride makes us greedy. We want to keep to ourselves all the praise we receive for doing things well, instead of passing it on to God. So we become more and more swollen with our own importance.

One way to pray through our pride is to use a method I have mentioned earlier: putting what we are thinking into words, so that we see clearly how ridiculous we are: "I really think I am much more advanced spiritually than most." Or, "I am truly generous; other people are so uncommitted!"

Back to the Pharisee again!

But God takes us by surprise in the way he responds to our bursts of self-congratulation. He doesn't say, "Be quiet, you idiot." He shares our gladness that something has gone well. But then he says to us, "This thing you're good at— haven't you noticed that it's a gift I've given you? If you're not careful you'll damage it by clutching it so tightly. You won't leave any room for me to do my work in you, if you are so cluttered up with your own achievements. Let go a bit!"

Once we recognize our pride, we can begin to pass on the credit and acclaim to God. When our pride has been deflated, we feel relieved that we don't have to defend a false image of ourselves anymore. Nor do we need to fear criticism or making mistakes—at least for the moment. Pride does have a way of creeping back unawares.

Humility is an elusive virtue, because as soon as we think we've got it, we've lost it. If we don't know whether we are humble or not, that's a good sign!

* * *

"The things that we love tell us what we are." Thomas Merton[8]

> O LORD, *thou hast searched me and known me!*
> *Thou knowest when I sit down and when I rise up;*
> *thou discernest my thoughts from afar....*
> *and art acquainted with all my ways.*
> *Such knowledge is too wonderful for me;*
> *it is high, I cannot attain it.*
> *Search me, O God, and know my heart!*
> *Try me and know my thoughts!*
> *And see if there be any wicked way in me,*
> *and lead me in the way everlasting!* Psalm 139:1-3, 6, 23-24

TWENTY-NINE

Self-Consciousness

*Our attempt to live a "good Christian life" is not without
its hazards. One is pride; another is self-consciousness.*

*Paradoxically, we are more likely to become the person
God wants us to be when we forget about our own "spiritual progress" altogether.*

T HE UNFORTUNATE CENTIPEDE is the object of much ridicule.
In addition to the story related previously portraying
him as a conceited twerp, another tale tells about a centipede
who was perfectly mobile until someone asked him how he
managed to walk with so many legs. As soon as he thought
about which leg came after which, he began to trip all over
himself. [9]

A similar danger besets prayer. Trying to live prayerfully
throughout the day can make us so self-conscious about every thought, word, and mouthful, that we lose our vision of
God. We will find him more readily by losing ourselves in
our surroundings than by analyzing our every response to
those surroundings. An incident which I experienced in a
barn, of all places, might illustrate this.

During a family vacation some years ago, we were potter-
ing around a farm. My children wanted to watch the cows
being milked, and the farmer agreed, on condition that we

stood completely still and quiet; a disturbance might upset the milking process. We stood in a line at one end of the milking area, rapt in silent attention.

"This is just right for prayer," I thought to myself, and I began to concentrate on inner quiet so that I could bring prayer (as I thought) into this pastoral setting. While I was busy trying to be holy, my eye fell on a notice pinned on the wall behind a large black and white cow: "Careful! Number 16 kicks when tickled."

Laughing to myself, I realized how absurd my self-conscious effort to pray had been, as if I could make this scene prayerful by my own spiritual technique. What I had to do was watch the activity around me, listen to the cows, smell the smells, and relish this splendid corner of God's creation.

Self-consciousness can cling to us like sticky candy, but it melts of its own accord if we turn our attention toward God and his world—and enjoy the cows, or whatever comes our way!

* * *

The quest of the self which God has meant each of us to be, is like the quest of happiness (which is indeed much the same thing)—it is not found by looking for it. Austin Farrar [10]

THIRTY

The Same Old Sins

Sometimes we wonder if we will ever stop committing the same old sins. In this we are in good company. "I do not do the good I want," wrote St. Paul, "but the evil I do not want is what I do." **Romans 7:19**

The cock didn't stop crowing the day Peter denied Christ, either for him or for us. Redemption is a long, slow process, and the closer we come to God, the more deeply we dig into ourselves, finding layers of rottenness we had not known were there.

T O FALL INTO THE SAME OLD FAILURES yet again is a terrible blow to our pride. We thought we were beyond such things. Or at least we hoped that God was changing us for the better.

He probably was—but not in the way we expected. Often the transforming work we have asked him to do leads us into chastening experiences we hadn't bargained for. Instead of being wonderfully freed from all selfish desires, we find deeply-rooted sins coming to the surface, sins which need to be confessed again and again. Reluctantly, we admit that we are not yet the kind of person we wish we were.

But we can take heart. The very fact that we are looking for God and trying to follow him means that we have, in a sense, already found him. We do not have to pass a test of moral virtue before we can be close to God.

The journey toward God is a spiral, not a straight line. We are not presented with a list of sins, to be overcome one by one, in a steady process leading to perfection. We will inevitably encounter the same weaknesses and commit the same wretched sins as time goes on. But we are a slightly different person each time it happens. Whenever we confess our repeated failures to God, his love penetrates us a fraction more deeply.

We naturally feel disheartened that we continue to let God down. But this should not stop us from trying. Each mistake healed and forgiven is a step toward union with Christ, even though we cannot see much progress ourselves.

Imagine someone in the opposite situation. This person has just experienced a dramatic Christian conversion and assumes that he has "made it" spiritually, not realizing that he is just beginning. What happens? Perhaps he is so discouraged when he recognizes his real condition that he gives up the whole business as a hoax. Or else he develops a false complacency ("I'm okay; I've made my decision for Christ, so I don't have to worry now") and settles down into a mediocre discipleship involving neither pain nor growth. In such a person the hidden, selfish motives and buried resentments remain untouched and therefore unhealed.

This is not to say that being a sinful Christian is a good thing! Paul faced a similar distortion of his teaching when some people from Rome challenged him: "Are we to continue in sin that grace may abound?" (Romans 6:1). Of course not!

But God can work *through* the chaos of our human failures, to bring new goodness that we would never have imagined. It is right that our sinfulness should distress us. Sin damages other people and ourselves only too obviously. But at the same time, we can grow through our errors, if we ask God to teach us more about ourselves, purify our desires, and make us more dependent on him.

When offered to God, the mess of our life is redeemed.

* * *

A Prayer with a Candle

My Lord and my God—
thank you for drawing me to yourself....
Lord,
You have told us that the pure in heart shall see God
—the single-minded
who do not try to serve two masters,
who have no other gods but you.
Keep the burning of my desire for you as clear and steady as the
flame of a candle
—a single, undivided focus of attention,
a steady offering of the will.
Let my whole being be filled with your light
so that others may be drawn to you.
Let my whole being be cleansed by the flame of your love from
all that is contrary to your will for me,
from all that keeps others from coming to you.
Let my whole being be consumed in your service,
so that others may know your love,
—my Lord and my God. **Margaret Dewey**[11]

THIRTY-ONE

Forgiveness Is a Choice

Being forgiven is not like going to the dentist for a filling so that we can eat again without pain; nor is it like fixing an automobile, so that it can run on its own.

Forgiveness is a process which we need all the time, not only to cleanse us from past sins, but also to make us more like the person we are meant to be—in God's image. This is what salvation is all about.

I OFTEN WONDER WHAT went on inside Zacchaeus, the unpopular little tax-man from Jericho, before he met Jesus (Luke 19:1-10). Perhaps he had already begun to wish he could shake himself free from the web of double-dealing and deceit in which he was trapped. If he refused to support the Roman government, he would lose his job; he must feed his family! If he stopped cheating, everyone would assume he had some ulterior motive. And to admit to the slippery tactics used by all tax-collectors would lose him the last few friends he had in the trade.

Maybe he longed, underneath it all, to live generously and openly, and to find real friendship and trust. Smatterings of Jesus' teachings must have circulated around Jericho. And now that Jesus was approaching, Zacchaeus wanted to get a bit closer to this figure whose ideas drew him so powerfully, in spite of himself.

So the drama began, with the familiar story of Zacchaeus sitting up in a sycamore tree, well hidden (as he thought) from the ridicule of his neighbors. Then Jesus astonished everyone by stopping and looking up: "Zacchaeus, I'm going to have dinner with you today!"

We can hardly imagine Zacchaeus' mixed reaction of delight and embarrassment at this moment. And then the joy and exhilaration when he finds the freedom to give back four times the value of what he has extorted from people and share the rest of his wealth so generously.

Zacchaeus found something infinitely more valuable than money. Because he was willing to open the door to Jesus, Zacchaeus was a different man. Jesus had accepted him and loved him as he was. This is what enabled Zacchaeus to discover his real self.

There are many ways of praying with this story. One is to use your imagination.

Be Zacchaeus; climb a tree and hope nobody sees you. Watch Jesus walking toward your tree; watch him looking up at you, and see all the crowds staring at you too. Listen to Jesus inviting himself to your house. Let him come home and sit down with you. What happens next?

Or you can ponder the way Jesus dealt with Zacchaeus. He didn't come storming into Zacchaeus' house, banging on the door and sweeping in with a tirade of condemnation. He waited until Zacchaeus had freely chosen to look out for him. He entered his house as a guest. And he transformed Zacchaeus by sitting down and eating with him.

If we were forced to love God, it would not be love. God enables us to make our own free and generous response.

* * *

Lord, I know you take me as I am;
but I want you to make me
what you would have me to be. **Richard Harries**[12]

"Behold, I stand at the door and knock; if any one hears my voice and opens the door, I will come in to him and eat with him, and he with me" (Revelation 3:20).

THIRTY-TWO

You Can't Keep Your Hands Clean

Christians are not sinless mortals floating around in an otherwise sinful world. We share the fallen human condition, and bear a corporate responsibility for the apathy and cruelty which damage so many people.

We are called, not only to serve Christ by standing up for what is right and loving, but also to bring to God the mess and muddle of the world, of which we are a part.

BEING A CHRISTIAN IN THE MIDST OF OUR WORLD is challenging, even in the best of times. Other people's standards and values can vary radically from your own.

I know of a woman named Jan who spent a weekend with her husband and several others at a luxury hotel, compliments of her husband's firm. Jan enjoys life and was looking forward to that weekend, but something about the experience sickened her.

A committed Christian, Jan's whole life was geared to finding ways of giving hope to distressed and underprivileged people.

During the weekend she suddenly found herself experiencing a nauseating glut of luxury. She felt miserable at the way other members of the party seemed to complain about inconveniences more than to enjoy the experience. For herself, she could not shake off a feeling of waste and extravagance, but she chided herself for being judgmental.

Her main sensation was loneliness, because everyone seemed so preoccupied with things that mattered little to her. At one level she and her husband belonged to that world, but, at another, they did not. She did not want to be a kill-joy or to take a puritanical stance against everyone else. Yet she wondered if her silence was somehow compromising her belief that luxury is a privilege, not a right, and that the good things of the world are enjoyed by sharing and not by grasping.

Many Christians face a similar dilemma, finding themselves in a tough, competitive world in which certain fundamental values differ greatly from their own. This is not to say that business and industry are evil in themselves, or that it is wrong to make a profit! But difficult questions arise if you have to work in a situation where financial gain is given higher priority than human safety; or where your firm exploits those who are desperate for jobs by forcing them to work very long hours and threatening to fire them if they refuse to do so.

How is a Christian to cope with this kind of situation? Many would like to escape, feeling that they are compromising their standards simply by being part of that world.

Yet none of us will ever escape to a "perfect Christian environment." We can't keep our hands clean. Our calling is to be in the world, though not of it. And that often means sticking it out where we are, not turning a blind eye to corruption, but praying faithfully for the discernment to know when to speak out, and when simply to be there, as Christ's leaven in the dough.

Jan's uncomfortable feeling in a velvety hotel lounge is a parable of the tension facing all Christians. As the author of the Letter to the Hebrews says, "Here we have no permanent home, but we are seekers after the city which is to come" (13:14, NEB). We belong to two worlds at once, and this is a tension which we cannot avoid. We share the sinful condition of all human beings. But we have been touched by a vision of something else, the joyful simplicity and generosity of Christ.

The answer is not to escape from one world into the other, but to remain uncomfortably in both, though prepared to face the cost when loyalty to God makes conflict with our fellows inevitable.

When we allow our anger or bitterness to hurt other people, we are adding to the destructive energy which leads to violence and war in the world. When we look at the pollution of the earth and the plight of the starving, we must remember that there is in each of us a small part of the blindness, greed, and selfishness which cause these things on a global scale.

So we need to expose to God the evil in ourselves, not only for personal forgiveness, but also as prayer for the healing of our violent and ravaged world.

In her booklet *Creative Suffering*,[13] Iulia de Beausobre talks about a traditional Russian Christian figure, the "holy fool," whose vocation is to mix with the outcasts of society. He lives with rogues and eats with beggars, so that he can participate in their life and offer it to Christ for healing and redemption *from the inside*. This, too, could become a parable for us.

In the days when I took my young children to school, the early morning rush at our house was anything but peaceful. It was easy to become irritated as the children ran around hunting for library books and swimming gear, falling over each other in the process. I remember on more than one occasion speaking sharply to my youngest for dancing around under my feet when I was trying to get everyone organized. After taking them to school, I would come home heavy-hearted at having given the children such a poor start to their day, and annoyed with myself for being so thoroughly bad-tempered.

It helped me to talk to other young moms, to discover that their early mornings were often the same. Familiar themes kept coming up: tiredness, frustration at the seeming impossibility of ever getting organized; anxiety about the children's day; and annoyance when people didn't immediately do as they were told!

Shake all these ingredients together in a busy parent on a rushed morning, and—POP—the cork will fly out. Even so, we can pray for each other from the middle of the tears and the mess, because we are all in the same boat.

* * *

Abba Father,
   With you, in my sinfulness,
Offering the world.
   With you in my weariness,
Offering the world.
   With you in my need of you,
Offering the world.
   With you in unbounded trust,
Offering the world.

THIRTY-THREE

From Self to Silence

*Silence can be an effective weapon against our sinfulness.
When we are before God in the stillness, we have no words
behind which to hide. Because we are empty-handed and
exposed, the Holy Spirit can penetrate the deepest parts of
our conscious selves.*

O UR *SELVES* ARE VERY NOISY: greed and ambition clamor
for attention; temptations clatter away; resentment rattles on. Part of praying involves letting go of this noise and
giving it into the hands of God. In return, God offers us a gift
of silence, in which our hearts and wills can be purified.

An experienced teacher tells me that one of the best ways
to calm and quiet a class of young children is to speak softly.
The kids all strain to hear, and then quiet down as a result.

We can apply the same method to our jangling selfishness.
Listen! God is whispering your name and saying, "Be still,
and know that I am God" (Psalm 46:10).

When we become quiet with God, he touches the roots of
our desires and actions. In the stillness we can lay ourselves
open to being transformed by his all-pervading mercy and
love.

A WAY TO BECOME STILL

Sit in a comfortable but not floppy chair.

Say slowly and thoughtfully the first two verses of Psalm 63:

O God, you are my God:
  early will I seek you.
My soul thirsts for you, my flesh longs for you:
  in a dry and thirsty land where no water is.

Say it again. Then repeat a few of the key words:

O God, you are my God...
My soul longs for you...

Repeat these phrases several times, until you feel that they are becoming part of you, sinking from your head to your heart like water into a dry plant.

O God, you are my God
My soul longs for you...

When you are ready, let the prayer become even shorter: *My God*, or, simply, *God*.

Let yourself enter into the silence, using the name of God to draw you again and again into his presence, which is beyond words.

When distractions come (which they will), offer them to God and then let go of them, returning to the full verse or to the simpler words, so that they can lead you back into silent communion with God. Numerous passages from the Bible can be prayed over in this way.[14]

* * *

"We seek 'a laying aside of thoughts, a progressive self-emptying, a self-noughting, that we may be filled with an all-embracing sense of the Divine indwelling. He must increase but we must decrease ...'" Bishop Kallistos Ware[15]

"Silence... prepares the way for the union of the soul with the will of God" (Rule of the Society of the Love of God).[16]

THIRTY-FOUR

Distractions in Prayer

When our prayer time has been invaded by thoughts about everything under the sun, we feel annoyed with ourselves for letting in so much mental chatter. We may be tempted to give up praying altogether and leave prayer to the "experts." But to do so would be a sad mistake. Everyone has distractions. Instead of letting them destroy our confidence, we should take hold of them, and then hand them over to God.

Y OU HAVEN'T FAILED AT PRAYER simply because you daydream about last night's television program or tomorrow's meetings during a quiet time with God. You are normal. What matters is that you have made space to be with God in the first place, and that you genuinely *want* to give him all your attention. That desire counts more than anything else.

Of course, distractions are not to be encouraged. I am speaking about times when you are doing your best to pay attention to God but are having difficulty doing so.

Distractions come in all shapes, sizes, and colors. Any great worry or unhappiness that weighs upon us is bound to dominate our mind during prayer. The main point of this book has been to explore how we can bring such troubles into our praying, rather than trying to pray *in spite of* them.

But at other times a welter of minor concerns bombards our minds. Sometimes it takes us a while to realize what's happening. The vital moment comes when we perceive that we have wandered away from concentrating on God. A distraction is only sinful if we deliberately continue it for our own pleasure, because to do that is to put other things before God.

So what do we do with our chatterbox minds?

Some would say that distractions should be banished by sheer willpower. I do not like that approach, first because suppressed thoughts tend to recur in any case, and second, because this method drives our distractions away from God, as if there were certain areas in life outside the orbit of his concern.

I find that it is best to make the distraction into a prayer, by turning my face back to God, and bringing with me the thing that has come to mind. It is like turning around to face the sun again. However small or petty, the distraction can be put to good use when I hold it in the stream of God's light, in a brief act of penitence, thanks, or intercession, or as a request for help. Then I can gently but firmly let it go.

Giving God our distractions is like handing over a parcel to someone else when we need to have our hands free. In most prayer times we will need to do this more than once.

The reason we feel guilty about distractions is that we know we are not giving God our full attention. It's right to be concerned about this. But most distractions are not sufficiently important for us to become too agitated over them. Absolute, unbroken concentration is very rare this side of eternity.

We don't apply such rigorous standards to ourselves in other circumstances, such as visiting someone in the hospital. As we chat or sit quietly beside our friend's bed, our mind may wander at times. But that doesn't alter our basic desire to pay attention to our friend. We won't be plunged into guilt if we happen to think about our journey home or the things we hope to accomplish during the rest of the day.

Similarly in prayer, the essential thing is our underlying intention to be with God. If we are doing our best to turn our attention to him, the odd distraction won't matter much. Instead of becoming tense and irritated when memories and thoughts run through our minds, it is better to treat them lightly. A short word or phrase, such as "Abba Father," or "My Lord and my God," or the name "Jesus," can help draw our attention back into line.

Far more dangerous is the distraction of spiritual pride: "I'm doing rather well at prayer!" That is the biggest distraction of all, and we need to turn our attention quickly from our own imagined progress and back to God.

CARS AND POTS

A friend of mine prays regularly in a small chapel, where you can always hear the traffic outside. When the noise becomes a distraction, she uses it as a reminder to pray for people she knows who are traveling, especially for a man in her church whose job involves a lot of driving. So a sound which could be annoying is turned into something positive.

It is said that while St. Francis was praying one day, his eye fell on a small pot which he had made. When he realized that his mind had wandered, he picked up the pot and smashed it. If I followed that principle in my living room, there would be precious little left! Daring to disagree with so great a saint, I think I would prefer to give thanks for the pot, before turning back to God.

I have some rather lopsided but extremely precious clay pots and figures which my children made for me at school. If my eye wanders onto those, the children can be brought into my prayer, in thankfulness and intercession. Then... let go!

* * *

"When a soul is completely given to Christ... there is a complete quieting of self. Only in the willingness to be conformed to God's will can true silence be found. Stillness of mind leads on to stillness of soul... so that the soul may be the true mirror that reflects the light of God." Mother Mary Clare [17]

O Holy Spirit of God—
come into my heart and fill me:
I open the window of my soul to let thee in.
I surrender my whole life to thee:
Come and possess me, fill me with light and truth.
I offer to thee the one thing I really possess,
My capacity for being filled by thee.
Of myself I am an empty vessel.
Fill me so that I may live the life of the Spirit,
The life of Truth and Goodness,
The life of Beauty and Love,
The life of Wisdom and Strength.
But, above all, make Christ to be formed in me,
That I may dethrone self in my heart
And make him King;
So that he is in me, and I in him,
Today and forever. Amen.[18]

Part Three

Praying with Misfortunes, Fears, and Frustrations

"The choice before the Christian is not whether he shall suffer or whether he shall not, but whether, given suffering, it shall be enlarging and enriching to the Body of Christ, or dwarfing and stunting." **Robert Llewelyn**[1]

"Blessed are they whose strength is in thee; who going through the vale of misery use it for a well."

Psalm 84:5-6, Book of Common Prayer

THIRTY-FIVE

Who Shakes a Fist at God

No easy explanations can be given to parents of dying chil-
dren or to the victims of horrible accidents which maim
and kill innocent people.

Christianity is not about rescuing God from blame in
the face of disasters; it is a way of living through our hell
with him. And that means absolute freedom to express our-
selves to God when we need to, with all our anger, frustra-
tion, and grief.

H UMAN BEINGS, with the capacity to love and rejoice and
laugh, have also wept and mourned and beaten the
ground in despair and anger all through history. The Bible itself contains several examples of people who raged against
God over their misfortunes.

"Thou hast made us like sheep for slaughter," complains
the psalmist, "the taunt of our neighbors, a laughingstock
among the peoples. All this has come upon us, though we
have not forgotten thee" (Psalm 44:11-17).

The great prophet Jeremiah, in one of his most despairing

moments, even called God a "deceitful brook" with "waters that fail" (Jeremiah 15:18).

We, too, need to be confident enough to pour out our feelings to God when misfortune strikes. Stiff devotional upper lips are definitely out.

Some people seem to think that the purpose of Christianity is to clothe everything unpleasant in holy language. For instance, instead of dying, people have simply "gone to a better place" and the sick have "joined the band of martyrs" and all misfortunes are "little things sent to try us."

I cringe when such ideas are forced on people who are facing tragedy. I was sixteen when my mother died, and I remember how it grated when a woman grabbed my arm and said, "Don't cry, dear; Jesus wanted her."

When people are at their most vulnerable, the last thing they need is to be told how to think. Instead, they need to be accepted as they are and given space. This is how God treats us, and we misrepresent him if we try to force others to accept pious interpretations of life's difficulties.

This is not to degrade Christian insights into suffering. It is important for us to think through our pain in the light of God's purposes. But that comes later. The first basic need is to be absolutely open and honest with God.

A pastor who counsels the bereaved[2] has observed that inner healing takes place in many people once they are able to give vent to their anger with God and then let go of it. At first, such people feel stunned and disinclined to pray. But when gently encouraged to pour out all the bitterness inside them, they often feel relieved, because the worst had been said. Instead of saying, "I can't pray," their misery has itself become a prayer.

Some of these people were surprised to experience a sense of profound peace. One described this experience as being "wrapped in love, in spite of the pain." [3]

If we insist on being politely insincere with God, we will

only construct a wall between ourselves and him. Finding easy explanations for suffering may keep God theologically respectable, but we are only protecting the idol of a safe and predictable deity, and losing touch with the real God in the process. You cannot let God off the hook! Don't be afraid to tell him so. He can take it; he always has.

* * *

"Both the people who are dying and their friends and relations and lovers must be free to express all their negative feelings and be angry with God if they want to. Often when you've expressed something it loses its power.

"And it's often by getting into anger that you find the real cause of many problems that have existed between you and the dying person. Because death is coming, we sometimes see families resolve problems in a short time; you move fast in a crisis and it's much easier if everyone is being honest" (Dame Cicely Saunders, A Pioneer of the Hospice Movement [BBC Radio 4, September 27, 1987]).

Who Shakes a Fist at God

Job looks craven:
Why didn't he fling the crockery?

Elijah under the furze bush fell to depression,
Hungry after running.

Jonah wanted it both ways:
Denunciation of Nineveh,
And the destruction of Nineveh.

Then, as cancer burgeons
Like weed; when the long
Fracture of infidelity stings the heart;

Or we get fired; or somewhere
A child dies against reason,

We'd lie, Lord, on the floor
And shriek; or throw a thick fist
At your love.

Love?
The dreadful sweat
Among old olives came out as
Bravery, elated mercy.
"I have," you affirm, "been already there,
Am acquainted with the hot finger of Providence,
How it feels,
From bruise
Through to blossom.

"I am there now." John P. White

THIRTY-SIX

Through and Beyond Our "No" to God

People are understandably cautious about the idea of saying no to God. It sounds as if we are saying that it is all right to defy and disobey him, or to turn our backs on him when we feel like it.

Obviously that is not what we mean. But if an overwhelmingly negative feeling is all we have, it is better to give that to God than to give him nothing at all. The very act of letting God have our "no" is, paradoxically, a kind of assent, a way of saying, "Here you are. This is me at the moment. You can have me as I am, filled with rebellion, misery, panic, and all. At least I won't hide anything from you."

"NO!" THAT'S HOW MOST OF US respond to terrible news, in numb and horrified disbelief.

A distraught wife sobs at the head of a mine shaft after a disaster below; a shy and lonely man learns that his closest friend has only two months to live; a father tries to take in the news that his daughter has been brutally raped. When tragedy strikes, we should be able to shout out our "no" to God, along with a whole flood of emotions.

I come back again and again to Jesus' struggle in the Garden of Gethsemane. Even he wanted to say no: "Father, take this cup away from me." Thank goodness the Gospel writers were honest enough to record this agonized prayer. It would have been so easy to gloss over it as an embarrassment, to give the impression that Jesus strode out through the olive trees to meet the soldiers without batting an eyelid. Jesus' "no" reveals the cost of what he eventually accepted. His identification with our misery is anything but a confidence trick.

Once we recognize and articulate the "no" which wells up inside us, as Jesus did that night, we are given the strength to move on into the pain with God.

Acute crises are not the only factors that can make us want to say no to God. We may be exhausted by too many demands, or drained by a difficult relationship, so that we feel like saying, "I'm sorry, Lord, but I simply can't take this!"

But what happens after we have dared to put our "no" into prayer? Everybody's experience of God is different, of course. Some people find themselves in spiritual limbo for a while, conscious that God is there, but unable to sense his presence. It takes courage and perseverance to go on praying and reading the Bible in such a situation, but it is well worth the struggle. Others feel an immediate sense of release and healing, because God has been with them at their weakest point and they now feel surrounded by his compassion. Yet others may find themselves wrestling with God, in a blind and painful struggle to come to terms with what is wounding them, like Jacob, who wrestled with the Lord all night (Genesis 32:22-32).

* * *

"I had to cut myself off, live a life of loneliness. When sometimes I overcame my fears, oh how brutally was I repelled by the redoubled realization of my bad hearing!...

"O God, thou lookest down into the depths of my soul, thou understandest me; thou knowest that the love of mankind and the urge to do good live within me....

"Permit me once again to experience a day of pure happiness! For so long now the inner echo of true joy has remained unknown to me. When, oh God, in the temple of nature and mankind, can I ever find it? Never? Oh, no, that would be too cruel to bear." (Written by the composer Ludwig Van Beethoven [1770-1827], when he was tortured by his deafness.) [4]

"...The bad news about Jennifer's illness really threw me for a week or two. I was rebelling and thrashing about, and feeling that if I stopped thinking about her for a minute (and tensing every muscle in my body in the process) I'd be letting her down. It almost felt like the *opposite* of prayer, and very selfish and exhausting....

"I had previously been trying to work on very simple 'stillness exercises' in meditative prayer. Now I found this almost impossible. But I spent some time just working on being still, and slowly bringing Jennifer and each member of the family into the stillness. It felt like the most strenuous task I'd ever attempted, but certainly helped...."

A Letter from a Friend

THIRTY-SEVEN

Falling to the Ground

"Falling to the ground" is a powerful image for a certain kind of praying. Some suffering does, metaphorically, knock us over, and there are no devotional formulas that will provide a quick fix to make everything all right.

When we have hit rock bottom, we cannot fall any further; but we can cry out to God from where we are—and perhaps discover that he is there with us, in the depths.

AN EPISODE FROM A RECENT COWBOY FILM sticks in my mind. An angry ranch owner shouts at one of his cowhands, "If your daughter thinks she's going to marry my son, she's as good as dead!"

At these words, the girl's father groans and falls to the ground.

"What's the matter with him?" asks the ranch owner.

A second man replies, "I'm a doctor. I've just had to tell him that his daughter has inoperable cancer. *She is indeed as good as dead."*

What struck me about this scene was the way it seemed absolutely natural for the father to fall down. People don't usually do that when they are distressed. But it made sense at that moment, as a far more real expression of the man's grief than any angry retort or violent gesture.

When my mother was dying, I often threw myself onto the floor and sobbed when I was alone in the house. Looking back, I can see that this expressed a fundamental need. At the age of sixteen, I felt as though I was falling with God into the darkness and pain of it all.

> ... Underneath are the everlasting arms....
> **Deuteronomy 33:27**

Jesus also fell to the ground. In the Garden of Gethsemane he fell on his face and prayed in anguish to his Father (Matthew 26:39). He must have fallen down, exhausted, while he was carrying the heavy cross-beam through the Jerusalem streets, because we are told that someone else had to bear it for him (Luke 23:26). And to crucify him, they would have pushed him down to lie flat while they drove in the nails. This extraordinary depth of vulnerability is at the heart of God and of the Christian gospel: "Unless a grain of wheat falls into the earth and dies, it remains alone; but if it dies, it bears much fruit" (John 12:24).

John the Baptist was thrown into the earth, imprisoned in the dungeon beneath Herod Antipas' palace. In a great agony of doubt he began to wonder if everything he had lived for was an illusion. Was Jesus really the Messiah after all? In desperation John sent a message to Jesus, "Are you he who is to come, or shall we look for another?" (Matthew 11:3).

Here was the great preacher, falling flat on his face into a hell of uncertainty, much harder to bear than the physical hardship of imprisonment. All he could do was put his questioning into words and offer it to Christ.

We should not be afraid to fall to the ground in prayer, either literally or metaphorically. It is a way of surrendering ourselves into the arms of God when hard things happen to us.

GOD IN THE RUINS

A terrible disaster overwhelmed the Welsh village of Aberfan in 1966, when a heap of coal slag slid down a mountain and half-buried a street, killing people in many buildings, including children in a school. One teacher died when she threw herself on top of one of her pupils to save his life. Many people said, "Where was God on that day?"

God was there, under the ruins, suffering with those people. And he was especially in that teacher, and all the brave people who risked their lives for the sake of others.

* * *

Out of the depths I cry to thee, O LORD!
Lord, hear my voice!
I wait for the LORD, my soul waits,
and in his word I hope. **Psalm 130:1, 5**

I am utterly bowed down and prostrate;
all the day I go about mourning.
I am utterly spent and crushed;
I groan because of the tumult of my heart. **Psalm 38:6, 8**

No matter how low we have fallen, God is beneath us, a bedrock underlying everything. We can never fall out of his care.

I love thee, O LORD, my strength.
The LORD is my rock, and my fortress, and my deliverer,
my God, my rock, in whom I take refuge....
In my distress I called upon the LORD;
to my God I cried for help.... **Psalm 18:1, 2, 6**

"When we are beaten down and lie flat with our mouths in the dust, hoping for hope... then we become aware that the whole meaning of our life is a poverty and emptiness, which, far from being a defeat, are really the pledge of all the great supernatural gifts....

"Freedom is found in dependence upon God....

"For God's love is like a river springing up in the depth and flowing endlessly through his creation, filling all things with life and goodness and strength" (Thomas Merton).[5]

THIRTY-EIGHT

In the Face of Mystery

Many painful things are a mystery, ranging from the cruel accidents of the natural world to the unreasonable behavior of the human race. We would feel better if God would only make himself small enough to fit into our tidy, logical schemes, so that we could explain everything and not feel so much at the mercy of irrational forces. But instead God takes the heart of the mystery of pain into himself.

SOMETIMES WE ARE TEMPTED to solve the mystery of suffering by saying that God deliberately inflicts it on us for our own good. Heaven forbid! The life and work of Jesus make it abundantly clear that God works for the healing of disease and the alleviation of human misery. The way a cut finger heals up is an example of the recuperative force which works in our bodies most of the time. When Christ heals, he harnesses and magnifies that same, God-given energy.

In Swaziland, where we lived for some years, babies often died of diarrhea because of dirty bottles and rampant viruses. Parents would sometimes say, "It is God's will." But I could not accept that. There is a difference between what God wills directly, and what he allows to happen because the world is what it is. For instance, if parents allow their teenage son to go on a bicycle ride, their permission includes the risk of his being knocked down and killed. But they do not directly will that outcome, and they are filled with grief if it happens.

So it is with God. His creation is a huge risk, and the delicate balance of conditions necessary for life to exist at all can go crazily wrong. We have bodies which feel pain, water which drowns as well as saves, fire which warms as well as wounds, and rocks which support us but can break apart in earthquakes. Yet God does not deliberately engineer human misery.

The fact that we ask why famines happen and babies die is evidence of hope. God could have made us heartless automatons; instead we are on the side of life and love—and that hurts.

God is always beyond us. We cannot summon him like a genie from a lamp, to give every story a happy ending, or to provide a rational explanation for every unfortunate circumstance. Suffering remains a mystery. What God has done, however, is to take into himself the consequences of our broken world, on the cross.

Our response to suffering can only be a mixture of anger and wonder. Faced with the irrational elements of human life, it is perhaps better during prayer not to try to work out reasons, but to remain silent in the darkness with God.

Death itself is a mystery. When someone dies we ask, "Where is he, where is she?" However deep our belief that life goes on, we still find it hard to grasp the fact that a person we love is not around any more.

"You'll get over it," people say. Bereavement is so easy to dismiss in the unwitting cruelty of kindly platitudes. But you do not "get over it" in the way that you get over the flu or a disappointing job interview.

Time, in my experience, does not heal the sense of loss, even if it heals the grief. Over the years, praying about the people we have lost becomes a mixture of good memories, painful longings—and silence.

* * *

"In the presence of mystery, what we must do is let the mystery be. Allow the mystery the fullness of its own being... allow God to be God." John Main[6]

THIRTY-NINE

No Certainty, No Control

One of the disconcerting things about misfortune is that familiar and comfortable elements of life are stripped away, and events move out of our control. This kind of wilderness experience can be very frightening. Yet God is there, in the chilly emptiness, even though we may not be aware of him at the time.

A CCIDENT OR ILLNESS CAN DEPRIVE you of ordinary, comfortable things, like going for a walk with your family or friends, or sitting down to a Christmas dinner together. Everything that has made you feel secure has been taken from you, and you worry for yourself and your family. With insecurity comes a sense of loneliness.

Words like, "Cheer up, you're in the wilderness with Jesus!" only make things worse. You just want to escape from such a bleak landscape, and it is important to share all your misery and anxiety with God.

But in the end, you must be able to accept the fact that this is your particular wilderness at present. It seems harsh to put it like that. Yet this is where you are, and this is where God is with you, not halfway down the road on some imaginary escape route, but here.

Nobody likes having control taken away from himself. As parents, we long to be able to do something when our children are unhappy or insecure; but sometimes there is absolutely nothing we can do, other than to suffer with them. For ourselves, too, there are moments when we wish we could press a magic button to put things right. But Christian faith is not about controlling events with the help of God (although some people appear to see prayer in this way). Prayer is the opposite of control—it is letting go of our lives and our will into God's life and will.

The very fact of being a Christian means that we live by faith and not proof (Hebrews 11:1); accepting a degree of uncertainty is part of our call. When Jesus sent his followers out in pairs to preach the gospel, he would not let them take any emergency supplies (Luke 10:3-4); managing without security was somehow essential to their task.

When trouble hits us, we may find we can no longer rely on ourselves, so we are thrown back onto God. It is then that he invites us to step out with him into the unknown.

In her book *Beyond All Pain,*' Dame Cicely Saunders describes the struggle of Enid at St. Christopher's Hospice:

Enid fought her way to peace, and we often had to battle alongside her. She found her profound dependence hard to bear, and could be difficult and demanding. Such struggles toward acceptance are often prolonged, as the same battle is fought over and over again.... She asked sometimes angry but honest questions of the God she deeply believed in and had served during her active life, and after a long battle she gradually accepted the reality of what was happening, and found the answer, which she has left us, dictated during the month before she died:

A friend and I were considering life and its purpose. I said, even with increasing paralysis and loss of speech, I believed there is a purpose for my life, but I was not sure what it was. We agreed to pray about it.... I was then sure that my present purpose is simply to receive other people's prayers and kindness, and to link together all those who are lovingly concerned about me. My friend said, "It must be hard to be the wounded Jew, when, by nature, you would rather be the Good Samaritan." It is hard. It would be unbearable, were it not for my belief that the wounded man and the Samaritan are inseparable. It was the helplessness of the one that brought out the best in the other and linked them together.

* * *

"He found him in a desert land,
*   and in the howling waste of the wilderness;*
he encircled him, he cared for him,
*   he kept him as the apple of his eye.*
Like an eagle that stirs up its nest,
*   that flutters over its young,*
spreading out its wings, catching them,
*   bearing them on its pinions."* **Deuteronomy 32:10-11**

I know
that when the stress has grown too strong.
    Thou wilt be there.

I know
that when the waiting seems so long,
    Thou hearest prayer.

I know
that through the crash of falling worlds
    Thou holdest me.

I know
that life and death are Thine
    Eternally. **The Reverend Mother Stuart**[8]

Lord, even when I cannot find you, you are still there.

FORTY

When Things Go Wrong

When we are doing what we believe to be God's will, we generally expect him to do his part and make sure that everything works out well. If things go wrong we get upset, and our confidence is shaken.

Yet part of our job as Christians is to taste what it is like not to be in a position of strength, especially if we are concerned to help the underprivileged. We find ourselves side-by-side with them—and closer to Christ—when we are vulnerable ourselves.

H OW EASILY WE FORGET that things sometimes went wrong for Jesus. When he came down from the stunning mountaintop experience of the transfiguration, he found his disciples struggling in vain to heal an epileptic boy (Mark 9:14-29). Even when he had just offered the bread and wine at the Last Supper, the disciples began bickering about which one of them was the greatest (Luke 22:24). That must have been the most poignant anticlimax in history.

Absolute power can be demonic, as Jesus knew when he was shaken by temptations in the wilderness. "Why don't you take the easy way?" whispered the devil. "Get popular quickly, impress everyone with a 'Superman' trick and jump off the Temple pinnacle. Coerce people into loving you, and avoid all the misunderstanding and pain. You can do it! Just worship me; do things my way, and you'll have the whole world at your feet!" (see Matthew 4:1-11).

But Jesus said no, choosing instead a way of limitation and suffering; and he is still with us in the misery of our weakness and uncertainty. The very fact of the Incarnation, God becoming man, reveals God's own mysterious vulnerability and self-emptying. It is not his way to provide us with a safety-rail; instead he invites us to walk on the water with him.

* * *

"For the sake of Christ, then, I am content with weaknesses, insults, hardships, persecutions, and calamities; for when I am weak, then I am strong." **2 Corinthians 12:10**

FORTY-ONE

Praying with Failure

Failure is a wilderness all of its own, an arid and comfortless ache of disappointment, humiliation, and frustration. Rational arguments like this do not help much: "We can't all shine. Everyone has strengths and weaknesses. You wouldn't want to succeed under false pretenses, would you?" Our heart is still as heavy as lead. We have, in a sense, been stripped by the experience, and stand helpless before God.

THOMAS MERTON ONCE WROTE, "The desert is the logical dwelling place for the man who seeks to be... solitary and poor, and dependent upon no one but God." [9] The miserable experience of failure brings us into such a desert whether or not we like it. For that reason it is a time when we can honestly say, "Lord, I am nothing; you are all."

Many people—especially Christians—impose upon themselves and others a crippling anxiety about "getting things right." Individuals struggle to live up to the straight-jacket of a so-called "ideal Christian life." Pastors are worn down by what appears from the outside to be failure and division in the church; congregations experience loss of confidence if numbers fall.

But the way of Jesus is not one of worldly success. His disciples constantly got their doctrine wrong, and let him down in the bargain. They misunderstood him (Mark 8:17), lacked faith (Mark 9:19), and abandoned him at the end (Mark 14:50). Yet their commitment during Jesus' earthly ministry and in the early church was crucial. It would have been a tragic loss if these men had refused to follow Jesus because they were afraid of making mistakes.

Of course we should try to be as generous and loving and true to Christ as we can. And of course we want the best possible outcome in our work for the kingdom of God. But the results of our efforts are God's, not ours. Christ liberates us from the need to rely on ourselves alone, and from the fear of failure, which can be such a heavy burden. As has often been said, God does not ask us for success, only for faithfulness. And when we offer our mistakes to God he sometimes uses them in ways that take us by surprise.

"The congregation was unanimous that it was the best sermon their pastor had ever preached. He was a bachelor, shy but extremely clever, and not always easy to understand. But this week everyone had listened. He was performing a baptism, and he began by telling people that he used to be terrified of small children.

"He particularly dreaded visiting his younger brother, who was the father of twins. Whenever he did, he used to trip over the children's toys because he was nearsighted. To make matters worse, he never knew what to talk to them about nor what presents to buy them.

"One day his brother and sister-in-law went out unexpectedly while he was visiting, leaving him to watch the twins. He did his best to play with the children and read to them, but he panicked when one of them spilled paint on the carpet. After a while, they began to argue and hit each other. When their parents returned, they were both screaming at the top of their lungs. He felt a complete failure—even though his brother later told him that the children liked his visits because he was so 'peaceful!'

"The pastor went on to say that he sometimes visited homes where parents felt inadequate. 'God has given you a challenging task, and you can't avoid mistakes, as I discovered in the fiasco with the twins. Children make you vulnerable,' he said, 'but they also make you alive.'"

* * *

"... *If any one among you thinks that he is wise in this age, let him become a fool... that he may become wise. For the wisdom of this world is folly with God....*

"*For all things are yours... and you are Christ's; and Christ is God's.*" 1 Corinthians 3:18-23

"The human heart longs for a true bonding, a true communion, which doesn't say, 'I'll love you if you are successful or clever or attractive.' We all yearn to be told, 'I love you because you ARE.'

"This is pure love, the real thing, like pure gold or pure water. And Christ loves us with that incredible, unconditional love" (Jean Vanier).[10]

FORTY-TWO

The Shapes of Fear

Fear takes many forms. Sometimes it is a permanent, though subtle part of our landscape. At other times it is so acute that it threatens to overwhelm us completely.

Praying through our fear does not take it away. But by looking it in the eye and naming it before God, we are more likely to find the strength to hold it rather than be held by it.

WHAT DO YOU FEAR? Illness? Nuclear war? Loneliness? Most of us struggle with fears and worries of one kind or another. Fear is natural, but we need to find ways of facing and harnessing it, rather than letting it dominate us.

Four primary shapes of fear can be identified. They are: the knife, the tight necklace, the cloud, and the coward. In addition, there is "positive fear," which is rather different from the others.

The "knife" is the most agonizing of all types of fear, a cruel thrust of dread in the stomach, when it seems that something terrible is happening: your child is dying, your husband is lost on a mountaineering expedition, you yourself may have inoperable cancer....

I call the second kind of fear "the tight necklace." It's almost as bad as the first; it's the choking panic that comes if you think you are about to be mugged, or your car is going to crash, or the building you are in is on fire. Lesser forms of this fear crop up at other alarming moments: when people hear a noise in the house and think it's a burglar, or when they suddenly panic in a lonely place.

The third kind of fear is like a "cloud" hanging over us. We imagine all sorts of awful things happening to our children or grandchildren. We are afraid of losing our friends, or of not being able to pay the bills. Such dark and chilly clouds cling heavily, almost physically at times.

Then there is the "coward." This kind of fear is a nagging anxiety about such things as unpopularity, fear of the dentist, or fear of facing up to a demand that we know we should meet.

POSITIVE FEAR

In contrast to the other types, which all have a negative aspect, there is a good kind of fear, springing from concern for others and compassion. You see examples of positive fear when people are anxious for the welfare of others. Being afraid to let God down or to betray our own conscience are also examples of this kind of fear.

Other people will identify different shapes of fear. Whatever they may be, it is useful to sort out our fears, as part of the process of recognizing and praying through them.

* * *

Lord, I am frightened. I am trying to pray, but my anxiety keeps taking over. Let my fear become my prayer, as I try to recognize it and give it to you. Deepen my trust, and help me to abandon myself into your hands.

FORTY-THREE

The Knife—Fear that Overwhelms

Some fear is so overpowering that we cannot hold or handle it ourselves. All we can do is stay still with God, in the middle of it. Even doing that is a way of facing the fear, however helpless we feel.

I NTENSE FEAR CAN DRIVE US, like a tyrant with a whip. I remember the sensation of being driven by panic as I walked blindly through hospital corridors when our three-month-old son was about to undergo heart surgery. Later, I went out into the street, bewildered that everyone around me was acting as though life was normal, even though my child was inside, fighting for his life. The fear monster held me in its iron jaw.

"I hate having to say this to parents, but I cannot promise that your baby is going to pull through." During the three terrible days after the doctor said that to us, the only prayer that made any sense was simply, "Oh God, don't let him die, please..."

For many hours the sense of fear almost paralyzed me, and I could only stand before God, numb and wretched. But there was one extraordinary moment when I sensed the power of love that was holding Andrew. I described this in an earlier book:

> "One morning while sitting with Andrew, whose body was a mass of tubes and wires linked to machines, I suddenly knew that he was in God's hands, whatever should happen. I realized that he was loved and held by God, whether he recovered from this illness or not.... This moment of heightened awareness lasted for only a short time. I soon became distraught again...."[11]

While Andrew's condition was critical, I both trusted God and didn't trust him, at the same time. Fear was never far away until the doctor was at last able to say to us, "He's got a good chance now."

I learned that praying through fear is a matter of hanging on to what we believe deep down, even when we can hardly convince ourselves that it's really true. Somehow we have to keep hold of God's promise to be with us, reaching out to him even when everything seems hopeless. "Trusting fear" or "fear-filled trust" sound like a contradiction in terms. But that is the way God's grace works in us when we are facing the acute stab of the knife of fear.

* * *

My God, my God, why hast thou forsaken me?
* Why art thou so far from helping me, from the words of my*
*   groaning?*
I am poured out like water,
* and all my bones are out of joint;*
my heart is like wax,...
But thou, O LORD, be not far off!
* O thou my help, hasten to my aid!* **Psalm 22:1, 14, 19**

O God, you know we are often filled with fear and fore-
    boding.
Give us courage, and deepen our trust.
You are a rock which nothing can shatter.
On you we place the whole weight of our lives.

Richard Harries[12]

FORTY-FOUR

The Tight Necklace— Should We Feel Afraid?

Sometimes people think that "real Christians" should never feel afraid, and that fear betrays a weakness of faith.

You do hear of outstanding individuals who plunge bravely into dangerous situations, knowing that Jesus is with them. But such courage is rare, and most of us do fear things like violence, illness, and insecurity. Trust would not be trust if we were not sometimes afraid.

"TIGHT-NECKLACE" FEAR, which we feel when something terrible might happen, is a perfectly natural reaction, and the obvious prayer is simply, "Help!"

I remember the boat ride my children and I once took off the south coast of Wales. We had boarded a small fishing boat with several other people. It was a blustery day, and as we went further out into the open sea, the boat was thrown around violently in the surging waves. We weren't the only ones who were frightened. As I looked around at the other passengers, fear was on every face. In the constricting sensation of fear, I remember trying to reassure the children, and praying continually under my breath, "Lord, help us."

Most of us do that in a crisis. And God was indeed there

that day, though I didn't feel it at the time.

But not all our fears are so acute.

Take my fear of the dentist. This superficial fear is overridden by a more sensible anxiety, that my teeth might fall out if I did not have the necessary fillings. And greater than both those fears is my trust that the dentist knows what he is doing. That confidence in my dentist's skill is what makes my fears bearable and gives me the courage (albeit flimsy) to face whatever treatment is necessary.

Although we should not stretch the comparison, such examples have spiritual parallels. They illustrate the way our fears vary in depth and value, and how they can be put into a wider context of trust in God.

Suppose someone needs to take an unpopular stand for what he believes to be right. If he is afraid of being scorned by others, that is "coward fear." But he may also be afraid of betraying the truth as he sees it, and fear the loss of his own integrity. When any of us face a similar situation, we have to pray that God will enable our good or "positive" fears to overrule the others.

* * *

Mikhail Kukobaka, Russian Orthodox Christian, has spent five years in Soviet psychiatric hospitals and eleven years in prisons and labor camps, because of his defense of freedom of speech. At the time of this writing, he is still in a strict regime camp, though great efforts are being made for his release[13]. In an open letter to the Soviet Minister of Health in 1979, which led to his re-arrest, he wrote: "I am frightened of prison, of camps, of lunatic asylums... but I am more frightened of lies, base behaviour, and my own participation in either of these, than of any prison. I am not ashamed to be called a prisoner.... I want to live according to my convictions."

FORTY-FIVE

The Cloud—What about the Future?

Anxiety about the future is the kind of fear that can swell out of all proportion to reality. Much of our fear is based on pure speculation, on things which might never happen. But we are only given grace to cope with the present moment; nobody can carry the burdens of next month and next year as well.

WE PICTURE ALL SORTS OF TERRIBLE THINGS happening in the future, events which may never occur: What if all our plans go wrong? How would we cope in such-and-such a crisis? What if...?

The world can seem a dangerous place into which to bring our children. We would not be human if we didn't worry at times. Yet, if we let go of undue worry about the future and concentrate on what God wants of us here and now, unexpected things can happen to enhance the quality of life in the present.

Numerous Christians can testify to this truth. Having given their time and resources generously in service to Christ, many people have found help and opportunities coming unexpectedly; they have known times of testing, but

God has not deserted them. They have discovered what Jesus meant by "seeking first the kingdom of God," and entrusting everything else to him: "Do not be anxious about your life, what you shall eat or what you shall drink, nor about your body, what you shall put on. Is not life more than food, and the body more than clothing? But seek first his kingdom and his righteousness, and all these things shall be yours as well" (Matthew 6:25, 33).

We can never strike a bargain with God or tempt him ("I'll do your will, if you'll look after me"). But giving our attention to what he wants in the present moment puts worry about the future into a different perspective.

This is not to say that we should avoid saving or planning ahead or taking out life insurance. Such things help us to deal with future needs and then to forget about them. But the significant question remains: is anxiety about the future so dominating our lives that we can spare little thought for what God is asking of us now?

* * *

If one day I should go out of my mind,
Lord, let me still be yours, even if I cease
to understand what being "yours" may mean.
I fear mental illness, change of nature,
the indignity of people saying, "Poor soul,
she's not the person that she used to be."
Lord, if I go insane,
let my condition be
an offering for the millions
of others who have faced
inner confusion and the loss of self.
O God, even my fear of "going mad"
is outstripped by your love
into eternity.

So help me to forget about tomorrow,
and concentrate on living in today.

"If we live, we live to the Lord, and if we die, we die to the Lord; so then, whether we live or whether we die, we are the Lord's" (Romans 14:8).

FORTY-SIX

The Coward—
Fear of Other People

The herd instinct is often too strong for us. We want to be-
long and be like everyone else, and we dread the moment
when eyebrows are raised and glances exchanged over
something we have said or done.

Sometimes people try to threaten or bully us into confor-
mity. It takes courage not to live up to other people's expec-
tations; it takes prayer to live up to God's—and to be the
person he intends us to be.

I ONCE KNEW A YOUNG WHITE SOUTH AFRICAN COUPLE who
lived in Johannesburg. Phil and Jane made friends with
several black people from work and from the congregation
where they worshiped. Black colleagues often came to have
supper with them.

As a result, they began to receive insulting letters from
other tenants in their block of apartments (who were all
white—by law), with insinuations that they might be forced
to leave. Jane and Phil kept on inviting their black friends to
their home, though by now their immediate neighbors
openly snubbed them.

These two people were profoundly prayerful. Their freedom sprang from being soaked in something greater than the desire to be liked and accepted. They were honest about their fear of harassment; but they also had something deeper from which to draw.

Their example reminds me of the story in Acts where Peter and John showed so much courage when they were hauled before the Jewish authorities. The high priest reprimanded them for teaching people about Jesus, and forbade them to do it again. With the glorious serenity of a person who was totally given to Christ, Peter replied, "We must obey God rather than men" (Acts 5:27-42).

A common factor among these brave people is that they are absorbed in the God who is stronger and greater than the things they fear. Their prayerful dependence on God gives them the courage and the freedom to discover their true selves.

PRAYING WITH THE FEAR OF CONFLICT

Ponder for a moment: do I help others by pretending to agree with them or by letting them rule my life?

Take the clashes between Jesus and the Pharisees. Suppose he had changed his mind and agreed not to heal on the Sabbath in order to avoid offending the authorities. Would it have helped anyone?

* * *

Lord, by your grace give me truthfulness, courage, and simplic - ity. Free me from the usual evasions which keep me from being my - self, and let me dare to receive the freedom you hold out to me.

"Fear not, little flock, for it is your Father's good pleasure to give you the kingdom" (Luke 12:32).

"... I am with you always, to the close of the age" (Matthew 28:20).

"... Do not fear those who kill the body,... fear him who, after he has killed, has power to cast into hell..." (Luke 12:4-5).

St. Paul writes, "Am I now seeking the favor of men, or of God?... If I were still pleasing men, I should not be a servant of Christ" (Galatians 1:10).

FORTY-SEVEN

Fear in a Wider Framework

Fear is not something to feel guilty about; it is something to put side-by-side with the infinitely greater power of God's love.

SOME TIME AGO I BECAME FRIGHTENED walking alone through a rundown section of London. Several unemployed youth were sitting on the walls outside their houses in twos and threes, sometimes not even talking, but just staring. Increasingly uneasy, I quickened my pace, wondering if they judged me a part of the system that aggravated their hopelessness and depression.

I came to a church, which I entered, since I had half an hour to spare before a meeting. No sooner had I sat down than several noisy teenagers followed me in and began cracking jokes at the back of the church. Then a street person smelling strongly of alcohol came and sat near me.

My discomfort grew. I wished I could escape to a safe place, somewhere I felt I belonged.

Then my eyes fell on the figure of Christ on the cross. And I found myself saying, "Lord, if I run away from all this, I am running away from you. You are here, in the middle of all this poverty and purposelessness—and laughter."

I gradually began to accept both my own reactions and the things around me. By saying yes to everything there, I was somehow saying yes to Christ. I realized that the street person and the teenagers at the back were not a threat, but fellow human beings, created and loved by God.

Mine was not an earth-shattering experience, nor was I suddenly free from all my fears. But I was given a glimpse, in spite of my thudding heart, of the fact that Christ offers us something greater than our fear. This experience taught me how loneliness can be turned into solitude when we are no longer so frightened.

A verse in the first Epistle of John sometimes makes people feel guilty about being afraid: "There is no fear in love, but perfect love casts out fear.... and he who fears is not perfected in love" (1 John 4:18).

We think to ourselves, "But I do fear certain things, so it must be my fault, and I must be lacking in love."

Such thinking is the result of a misunderstanding. The verse needs to be seen in the context of the preceding passage, which is about God's love for us (4:10). It is the "day of judgment" that we need not fear (verse 17), because God's love for us is so great. As long as God's love lives in us we have nothing to fear of his punishment (verse 18). Hence, "perfect love casts out fear."

It is true that the more we love God, the less we are ruled by fears for ourselves. On a human level, too, the more secure we feel in the love of other people, the less we fear a disagreement with them. But this is quite different from saying that it is sinful or unloving to be afraid.

The agony which made Jesus sweat blood in the Garden of Gethsemane must surely have included human fear. And Jesus lacked neither trust nor love. For him, as for us, certain things are indeed fearful. Yet for him, as for us, there is something stronger and deeper: the steady love of God, who sustains us through and beyond all our vulnerability.

* * *

A monk of the Egyptian Coptic Church described how he used to be afraid of wolves, when he was in his lonely desert hermitage. But then he realized that they, too, were creatures made by God.
They did him no harm.

> May I be without fear,
>   by night and by day.
> Let all the world be my friend.[14]

FORTY-EIGHT

Positive Fear—The Other Side of Hope

The fact that we fear many things is not totally bad. We only feel afraid because we have a basic sense that life is valuable, with a purpose and meaning that we want to protect. Like guilt, fear makes a useful servant but a bad master.

Praying with our worries is a sifting and sorting process, because God enables us to see which things really matter, and which we need to let go of.

FEAR CAN BE USEFUL when it prevents us from doing dangerous or foolish things. If a small child is completely fearless, we become rightly concerned for him: he might touch the fire, run into the road, or walk straight off a cliff.

Some of our anxiety for other people, or for issues which really matter, is "positive fear," and could be said to be the price of loving. Other fears are a form of selfishness which need to be discarded. Perhaps we are pinning too much hope on our job, reputation, or standard of living, and need to loosen our worried grip on these things. Perhaps our parental concern is in danger of degenerating into overprotectiveness. Praying with God about our uneasiness helps us to distinguish between the sensible and the not-so-sensible kinds of fear.

Some people are worriers by nature and need to let go of excessive misgivings; others are more happy-go-lucky, and should perhaps feel more anxiety, not less, about the things that threaten our human community. God is not going to change any of us into different people; but he can bring out our hidden capacity to rise above our weaknesses, so that we become "caring happy-go-lucky" people, or "brave worriers." Prayer is where our limitation meets God's greatness.

Many of our fears are part of the price of living in a marvelous yet dangerous world. To possess something precious is to risk losing it; sharing this planet with other people means that we might be hurt by them. We are never totally secure, but few of us would want to live in a perfectly safe and insulated box.

God's love is stronger than all our evil. We, the human race, did our worst at the crucifixion, and attempted to kill God in Jesus. Yet he rose from the dead, and is with us in a more far-reaching way than ever before. Absolutely nothing can beat him now. He is a bedrock of hope beneath even the worst of our fears.

Even the horrific prospect of a nuclear holocaust—a trauma so deadly that we can hardly imagine it—is contained within Calvary. The cross was God's own holocaust, the place where he was wholly burned out for us, and from it came the triumphant cry: "It is finished" (John 19:30)—"We've won!"

Many worries and fears are like the clouds that cover parts of the earth, which can be seen on those magnificent photographs of our planet taken from the moon. Viewed from a distance, we see that they are only part of a world far greater than themselves.

* * *

"Fear not, for I have redeemed you;
   I have called you by name, you are mine.
When you pass through the waters I will be with you;
   and through the rivers, they shall not overwhelm you;
when you walk through fire you shall not be burned,
   and the flame shall not consume you.
For I am the LORD *your God,*
   the Holy One of Israel, your Savior...." **Isaiah 43:1b-3**

FORTY-NINE

Doubt

Faith would not be faith without an element of doubt, any more than courage would be courage if we did not feel afraid. Praying with doubt is part of our searching and longing for God.

N O ONE CAN POSSIBLY GRASP everything there is to know about God. It is absurd to demand absolute certainty from anyone. On the contrary, it is those who have prayed and loved God most who have always had the strongest sense that he is unfathomable.

If we think we have a totally comprehensible God, we are in danger of idolatry, because we will try to contain him by virtue of our own definitions. That is to reduce him to a "thing" that can be held captive by our finite minds. Yet God is infinite and beyond us, so that religious experience must include an element of not knowing. As St. Paul says, "Now we see in a mirror dimly." "How unsearchable are his judgments and how inscrutable his ways!" (1 Corinthians 13:12; Romans 11:33).

Living and praying as Christians sometimes means persevering with a mixture of faith and doubt, and this can be very painful. We long for some final proof, to put an end to the uncomfortable challenge to our beliefs. Surprisingly, things which seemed a threat to our faith at one time can become a help later, in our search for a deeper understanding of God and his ways. The important thing is that we are open with him about our doubts, even when it is his very existence that we are questioning.

* * *

Lord, even you know what it is like to feel as if "God is no more," to wonder if what you've staked your whole life on is after all just an illusion. You know what it is like to keep going in the dark by a sheer act of will; to go on loving when there seems to be no response; to abandon oneself to a divine providence one can neither see nor feel. Lord, when it is dark and we cannot feel your presence, and nothing seems real any more, and we are tempted to give up trying—help us to know that you are never really absent—that we are like a little child in its mother's arms, held so close to your heart that we cannot see your face; and that underneath are the everlasting arms. **Margaret Dewey**[15]

FIFTY

Praying When You're Ill

When we are ill, we honestly don't feel like praying very much. Instead of trying to stick to our normal ways of spending time with God, it is a relief to discover another way of praying—a more passive kind, a letting go into God. It doesn't matter if we do not have much drive or energy of our own, because prayer is as much God's activity as ours.

WHAT SORT OF A GOD DO WE THINK WE HAVE?

When you are ill, nobody expects you to leap onto a train and go to work, or race around the house doing spring cleaning. Most people will understand that you cannot function normally, and so does God.

He knows how unwell you are feeling. He is not going to force you into practicing demanding forms of prayer, like some harsh Dickensian headmaster. Illness is supremely the time when we should "pray as we can, and not as we can't." [16]

A sick and weary body can express certain things that cannot be conveyed quite so deeply when we are hale and hearty. We are used to the idea that the body expresses praise or devotion in ordinary worship, by kneeling, standing, or sitting with the palms of the hands open. In the same way, the very act of lying down when we are ill can be a statement of trust and self-abandonment to God. Because we are physically weak we can only surrender ourselves into the Power greater than ourselves who is God.

Illness is an opportunity to discover something about the more passive side of praying. Our task is not so much to do things, as to be willing to let God work in us. This is true of all prayer, and is the paradox which made St. Paul say, "When I am weak, then I am strong" (2 Corinthians 12:10).

There is no single way of praying during an illness. Some people find prayers of relaxation helpful. But a friend who is in constant pain says that such suggestions make her want to scream. For her, trying to relax her body only brings the pain and discomfort into sharper focus, making it even more of an unbearable distraction to prayer.

We simply need to discover which of the many possibilities are best for us.

By far the most important thing is the fact that we even want to pray when we are ill. Our desire for God, however feeble and befuddled, is what matters, and the way in which we pray is secondary. For some people, the knowledge that they want to reach out to God is literally all they can manage. Often, these people need the prayers of others to help them to express their need for God and develop it further (a theme explored in the next section).

Single words such as "Lord," "Jesus," or "Abba Father" give us something to repeat and hang on to when nothing else is possible.

RELAXING IN PRAYER

The prayer of relaxation can be particularly useful to those who are exhausted or convalescing, or who suffer from a debilitating ache rather than an acute pain.

Lie still, as relaxed as you can. Put yourself into God's

hands. Starting at the top of your head, concentrate on relaxing the muscles all the way through your body, progressing slowly downwards: eyes, back of the throat, neck, shoulders, arms, and so on. As you do this, imagine that each part of you is melting, like ice in hot water. Let this melting become your self-abandonment into the warmth and healing power of God, whose love is flowing through you.

A simple prayer to use as you come to each part of your body is: "Jesus—my weakness into your strength."

HOLDING OR TOUCHING

Others may prefer to find ways of distracting the body by actually doing something. One possibility is to trace certain shapes with the finger.

David Adam's book, *The Edge of Glory*,[17] contains many "encircling" prayers and motifs in the Celtic tradition, which convey how we are surrounded by the divine love.

You could trace with a finger the shapes that accompany these prayers, before, after, or at the same time as praying the words themselves:

The Trinity
Protecting me
The Father be
Over me,
The Savior be
Under me.
The Spirit be
About me,
The Holy Three
Defending me.
As evening come
Bless my home,
Holy Three
Watching me.

As shadows fall
Hear my call.
Sacred Three
Encircle me.
So it may be
Amen to Thee.
Holy Three
About me.

The circle and the triangle remind us of the mystery that God's love is infinite and eternal, without beginning or end.

This Celtic trefoil is another motif which can be traced with a finger, using a prayer such as: "My Lord, My love, My life…" Simply looking at this figure, and thinking the words, might also help focus your attention away from bodily discomfort and onto God.

USING THE PRAYERS OF OTHERS

Old favorites like Psalm 23 take a lot of beating when we feel unwell:

The LORD is my shepherd,
    I shall not want;
    he makes me lie down in green pastures.
He leads me beside still waters;
    he restores my soul.
He leads me in paths of righteousness
    for his name's sake.

Even though I walk through the valley of the shadow of
    death,
  I fear no evil;
for thou art with me;
  thy rod and thy staff,
  they comfort me.

There are other helpful psalms in the ancient nighttime office of Compline, for example:

In thee, O LORD have I put my trust,
  let me never be put to confusion,
  deliver me in thy righteousness;
Bow down thine ear to me,
  make haste to deliver me;
And be thou my strong rock and house of defense,
  that thou mayest save me . . .
. . . Into thy hands I commend my spirit,
  for thou hast redeemed me, O Lord, thou God of truth.

                    Psalm 31:1-5, Book of Common Prayer

USING THE IMAGINATION

Some people find the imagination a useful tool in prayer.
  Picture Jesus healing people, and then see him walking toward you, looking at you with deep compassion, and
stretching out his hands toward you.
  You could imagine that Jesus takes both your hands in his.
Feel the warmth; the love; the sense of security, come what
may.
  There is another Celtic encircling prayer which you could
say as you imagine this:

I place my hands in yours, Lord,
I place my hands in yours.

I place my will in yours, Lord,
I place my will in yours.
I place my days in yours, Lord,
I place my days in yours.
I place my thoughts in yours, Lord,
I place my thoughts in yours.
I place my heart in yours, Lord,
I place my heart in yours.
I place my hands in yours, Lord,
I place my hands in yours.

FIFTY-ONE

The Prayers of Others

A hospital chaplain tells me that people often ask him to pray because they feel too ill to do so themselves. Praying either individually or in a group is an important way of helping sick people to be held in the love of God.

Furthermore, being ill can land you with a ministry to all the people around you who want to help.

I F YOU ARE ILL, and friends in the room are praying for you, your part is simply to surrender yourself into the hands of God, like lying in a safety net which is being held by other people. Let others say for you what you cannot say yourself, knowing that you are surrounded and soaked in God's love. Just by being there and consenting to this, you are part of the praying.

The most important thing to realize is that you are accepted and profoundly loved by God, however unsatisfactory or difficult your life. In that fact alone lies the heart of healing.

Christians involved in full-time ministries of prayer for healing usually say that many people are physically healed, but not all. We do not understand why. But what we do know is that God always blesses people through prayer, sometimes in unexpected ways.

Whatever happens to you, the essential truth, which nobody can take away from you, is that God loves you. Coming to realize that fact more deeply may itself be a step toward physical recovery.

This is a prayer for a friend to say for you:

> The weaving of peace be thine
> Peace around thy soul entwine
> Peace of the Father flowing free
> Peace of the Son sitting over thee
> Peace of the Spirit for thee and me
> Peace of the One
> Peace of the Three
> A weaving of peace be upon thee...
> ... Around thee twine the Three
> The encircling of the Trinity.[18]

Sometimes the best way for a friend to help is just to be present with the sick person, sharing his powerlessness and silence before God.

Having others pray for you while you are sick may, however, be a mixed blessing. On the one hand, the sensitive and faithful prayer of friends can be an invaluable help. But some people may unwittingly pressure you, so that you feel as though you are letting them down if you don't get better. I know a sick person who is surrounded by so many Christians full of zeal for God's power to heal, that they never give him space to say, "I feel dreadful," or a chance to pray through that feeling.

This is intercession gone wrong. Of course we should ask God for healing, and we should be open to whatever he will give us. Many people are healed, sometimes dramatically, in this way. But it is wrong to feel that physical healing depends on how much teeth-gritting "faith" we can muster. Such an approach is a distortion of Christ's healing work, and only adds a burden of guilt to the misery that sick people already feel. True faith is having the guts to come to God empty-handed, and to depend totally on him. It is not some feat of willpower, an attempt to convince ourselves that we will get what we want out of God, come what may. Healing depends on the will and grace of Christ, not on us.

Another approach is to try to see the lighter side of our predicament. The next time an overly zealous friend insists on laying hands on you and saying, with ever-increasing intensity, "O Lord, forgive this thy child for his lack of faith, and let him claim the total recovery you are definitely offering him, NOW!," will you try to see the funny side of it? Is it possible to send up your hurt and irritation on an imaginary air balloon, and to ask for blessing and the gentle touch of God's Holy Spirit, both for the person praying and for yourself?

If the truth were told, most of us aren't good at being with sick people. Either we say too much, or we are so embarrassed that we don't mention the very things the ill person wants to talk about. The prayers we say are often hesitant and stumbling. People who are ill may have their work cut out reassuring and putting at their ease those of us who are trying to help them!

Many people feel awkward at the thought of being prayed over when the clergy or other members of their church visit them in the hospital. I have a friend who was embarrassed when her minister stood by her hospital bed and prayed loud and long, just as the lunch cart was coming in. Apparently oblivious to the activity and smell of food around him, the pastor went on and on, eyes tightly shut. The nurse waved a plate of food at my friend and asked, by gesticulation, if she wanted any gravy. The food was cold by the time the prayer was finished.

Fortunately, that scenario is unusual. Hospital chaplains are usually sensitive to the needs of patients, and the vast majority of pastors will not impose themselves or their prayers on you.

It is precisely because they want to avoid causing embarrassment that many clergy wait to be asked before they pray with patients. If that happens, and you would like him or her to pray, do ask. It is sad to hear someone saying afterwards, "We had a good talk, but I would have loved a prayer."

Perhaps we can learn something from the approach of a friend of mine who was pastor of a tough inner-city church. He tells the tale:

> I went to see an old street-person, George in Ward 9.
>
> We talked a bit, and then I said, "Right, now I'm going to say a prayer."
>
> George retorted, "Oh no you're not! I don't . . . well believe."
>
> "Lie down and shut up," I replied. "God loves you whether you like it or not. You're not going to stop him!"
>
> After I had prayed, he held my hand in both of his for a long time....

That, too, is unusual behavior among the clergy! But it's a good story, and shows what can happen if barriers are overcome.

Receiving communion at home can sometimes cause people concern, and this again is why some pastors wait to be asked. Many people feel so awkward at the prospect of their pastor seeing them ill in bed that they think they could never concentrate properly on worshiping. But pastors are not embarrassed by your current state of weakness, any more than by the tears of the bereaved.

The fact that you have not attended church for a while need not prevent you from asking to receive communion at home either. Sometimes people who have drifted away from regular church attendance find that this sparks off a rediscovery of their faith.

Most people find communion at home far more relaxed

and undemanding than they had expected. You don't have to sing hymns, stand up, kneel down, or plow through long prayers for which you do not have the strength. My own experience of receiving communion, both in the hospital and at home, is of a gift, offered in an atmosphere of peace and gentleness.

"Part of something bigger" is a phrase I have often used in this book. It is particularly relevant when we are ill and other Christians are praying for us. Knowing that we are regularly remembered by individuals, groups, and congregations draws us into the prayer of the whole body of Christ.

Monks and nuns, especially those called to the enclosed life of prayer, are there to hold the rest of us in the healing love of God. That is their job. So it is good to write (or ask a friend to write) and request prayers when you are sick or facing some other kind of difficulty. Doing this will help you realize that you are part of the ongoing rhythm of worship which is the lifeblood of the church. You need to know that you are taken up into something which transcends space and time.

Tape-recorded hymns and songs can deepen this sense of belonging to the wider Christian community. I find the tapes of music from Taizé particularly helpful here.[19]

* * *

Christ be with me, Christ within me,
Christ behind me, Christ before me,
Christ beside me, Christ to win me,
Christ to comfort and restore me.

Christ beneath me, Christ above me,
Christ in quiet, Christ in danger,
Christ in hearts of all that love me,
Christ in mouth of friend and stranger. **St. Patrick (A.D. 389-461)**

FIFTY-TWO

Physical Pain

When we are in physical pain, the last thing we want to be told is that we should welcome it. It doesn't matter how useful pain is to doctors in revealing what is wrong with us, or how close we ought to be feeling to Christ in his suffering; we wish to be rid of our misery.

So far I have looked at ways of praying which help to focus our minds on God rather than on our own ailments. But it is also essential to come to terms with our physical state, and to make that a part of praying too.

I T IS THE MOST NATURAL THING in the world to ask God to free us from our suffering. We need not apologize to him for wanting relief; expressing our weakness and need is part of being ourselves and coming to God as his children. Although we may not receive exactly what we ask for, God will always give us himself in the midst of our suffering, however hellish it may seem.

Some years ago, when I was suffering from chronic headaches, my spiritual director advised me, "Make the pain your prayer." That was tough advice, but he was right. Following the principle of "protest and say yes," we need both to voice our complaints to God, and to deal with what is happening to us.

I hesitate to write about this, because I have never suffered prolonged or intense pain, except when giving birth; and then it was somehow different, because there was an obvious purpose and an end in view. I cannot imagine what it must be like to endure constant, severe pain. But from my experiences of headaches and back trouble, I know that pain can be utterly draining, dominating all thought and feeling. So it makes sense to make the pain itself our offering to God; we have nothing else to offer anyway.

On the rare occasions when I have been immobilized because of a bad back, I have never felt that I was making much progress with prayer. But that's not the point. The spiritual life is not about being an "expert" at prayer. What matters is that we keep looking in God's direction, rather than turning in on ourselves, which, of course, is one of the hazards of any sort of pain or illness.

* * *

"Lord, I give you my pain; it's yours too" is one prayer we can use, especially while looking at a figure of Christ on the cross. Or we can repeat a single name or word, such as "God," "Love," "Lord," or "Jesus," when we are hanging on to prayer by the skin of our teeth.

FIFTY-THREE

Nausea

Feeling sick is one of the deadliest enemies of prayer. Three queasy pregnancies taught me that! But even in the throes of an upset stomach we can discover something about being in the misery with God, rather than trying to find God in spite of the misery.

O NE OF THE HARDEST KINDS OF ILLNESS to pray with is the common stomach flu or general nausea. Since you're not desperately ill, you needn't summon vast reserves of courage to cope with your sickness. But you feel absolutely *awful*.

On many days I have felt so terrible that I have hardly given God a thought, let alone managed any conscious praying. On other occasions I remember feeling pretty angry with God for allowing sickness and diarrhea into his creation. (To my shame, I am capable of getting more worked up about this than about the serious diseases which ravage others.)

With my amateur knowledge of biology, I know that we all need bacteria to survive, and that the bug which makes me ill also has something to do with the conditions necessary for life. But such knowledge doesn't help much when I am feeling so awful.

So what about prayer? There will be the inevitable groaning and moaning to God, and asking to be relieved of this horrible feeling. Then what? How could there possibly be anything more? you might ask.

Believe it or not, two things do come to mind.

During one of my twenty-four-hour bouts of gastroenteritis, I tried putting a cross under my pillow. I wasn't sure how this would work out, but I found it surprisingly helpful. Lying in bed feeling dreadful, I could slip my hand up and get hold of the cross. This gave me an assurance that Jesus was there, in the misery, with me. He understood, he was close, and he could cope with my complaining and railing against God.

Something else that has helped me is to think about the fate of people in squalid refugee camps, who easily contract dysentery and similar diseases. I wonder what it must be like for them, being ill in a rough tent with no sanitation or running water?

On the wall downstairs I keep a bulletin board with names and pictures of people in various kinds of distress, such as famine, floods, and political imprisonment. Looking at it is a form of intercession. When I am ill in bed I can think about those pictures, especially one of a forlorn family in a refugee camp in Sudan, where hygiene is appalling, supplies scarce, and the water filthy.

My life is so different from theirs; and yet I share with people who are sick in those camps this terrible feeling of nausea. So I pray with and for them, offering my comparatively tiny sufferings as a prayer for them in their great misery.

* * *

Lord, hang on to me, because I don't feel well enough to hang on to you.

FIFTY-FOUR

Frustration and Humiliation

One of the things that can be so difficult about being ill is that you can't do everything you think you should be doing. Loss of independence is especially hard if you are the mother of a young family, and cannot look after your children. You feel as though your role and identity have been taken away from you.

It's also frustrating to lack the energy to enjoy your favorite pastimes. Lacking the drive or enthusiasm to do much, your spirits become low, as well as your body. Such times provide a real test of your willingness to let go of your dignity and achievements, and to put your trust in God instead of yourself. You have nothing to offer him but your helplessness; accepting this is hard, but to do so is to accept a chance to be purified—less of you and more of God!

I T IS EXTREMELY DIFFICULT to avoid being irritable and critical when we are unwell and other people are doing what we would rather be doing ourselves. For instance, I find it very difficult to control my temper when my back is acting up and my family often has to take over in the kitchen.

199

Self-pity is another stubborn demon to dethrone when we are ill. We think nobody understands, and we start to imagine that people resent having to do extra things for us. Either we don't have enough visitors, or people stay too long. "If so-and-so had been a little more thoughtful..." we say to ourselves.

In some ways self-centeredness is unavoidable when people are ill. Healthy people busy themselves with their jobs or domestic activities. But sick people often have to spend much of their time and energy figuring out how to cope, whether they have taken their pills, what the doctor will say next, and when they will feel better. That is the problem which has landed in their laps, and it is not their fault that so much of it concerns themselves.

Most long illnesses also involve an element of loneliness. Some people probably won't understand what you are going through; others will not be sympathetic for very long and will soon become more impatient than interested.

What we all have to watch, whether we have an earache or terminal cancer, is that we do not retreat into a miserable fortress of self, from which our only consolation is to take potshots at everyone in sight. Self-pity has to be seized by the scruff of the neck and given to God. He can deal with it, though we can't. When we ask for forgiveness, his mercy comes rushing out to meet us, and it is often the only thing that keeps us going.

The indignity of being unable to deal with one's personal needs is another of the miseries endured by those with serious illnesses. A friend with multiple sclerosis puts this vividly:

> To be washed and dressed and even the most intimate details of one's toilet done by somebody else; someone else decides what and when you shall eat and drink, and puts the cup to your mouth.... It takes every bit of humil-

ity you've got to keep from screaming, "Will you not pour that down my throat as if it were a sewer!"

These words come from a talk that this friend gave, very bravely, at a seminar on healing. She then went on to make a crucial observation:

Although I couldn't see it at the time, this is a share in our Lord's humility when he became man and suffered the limitations and indignities of being human.

In facing her situation, my friend has found a way of coping which is neither a resigned giving-in nor a grudging acceptance. She wholeheartedly loathes her illness, yet wholeheartedly accepts it, and has discovered Christ alongside her in the process.

Illness has a way of turning our worldly values upside-down. No longer are we productive, self-sufficient people. In fact, we can do very little that's considered useful. And yet our real value as human beings is not diminished in the least. To realize this can help us to discover that we matter to God because we are who we are, and not because of what we can achieve.

* * *

Lord, this is intolerable. I *am* grateful for all the people rallying around me. I couldn't manage without them. But I hate the fact that I need them. Teach me how to receive as well as give. Help me to use this maddening situation positively, as a chance to let go of my desire to be organized, competent, and always in control. Set my spirit free, knowing that I am infinitely valuable to you, even when I'm stuck here!

I pray for all those people who never have the satisfaction of getting a good job done, because of permanent illness, or unemployment, or because they are struggling to scratch out a frugal living under an unjust system. I pray for them, because I am—at least for the moment—one with them in this feeling of helplessness.

Jesus, I think of what they did to you in Jerusalem, stripping you of your clothes, nailing you to a cross. You have plumbed the depths of humiliation and weakness. You are in this with me, from the inside. I thank you for that.

We can be spiritually independent, even if physical independence is lost. **Dame Cicely Saunders** [20]

FIFTY-FIVE

In Great Suffering

I have a friend in a wheelchair, Anne, who developed muscular sclerosis after her husband committed suicide, leaving her with two young sons. Another friend, Mary, also with small children, suffers from a rare and debilitating tumor on her neck.

How do you pray in situations like theirs? On one level I simply don't know. I have no idea what I would do if I were in their shoes. But getting to know them both has taught me a lot about relying on the grace of God.

B OTH OF THESE WOMEN are Christians. Each has gone through periods of darkness, when she couldn't think straight, pray consciously, or find anything positive to hold on to. And both have shown tremendous courage.

Mary had radiation therapy, and was making a good recovery. But later on a further scan revealed that the tumor had not responded to the treatment, and was continuing to grow. She felt that she had been knocked over again just when she had begun to pick herself up. At this point she began to wonder if she could trust God any more. Paradoxically, it was a relief when she was able to acknowledge her discouragement and doubt and express her frustration to God.

Both my friends know what it's like to have hit rock-bottom. Their words speak volumes.

Mary said, "I reached a point where I stopped holding on to God any more. But I have discovered that when I can't hold on to him, he is still holding on to me."

In a talk from which I also quoted previously, Anne said: "God never anywhere promises to heal all our sickness, or magic away all our suffering. What he does promise, time and again, is *'My grace is sufficient for you'* (2 Corinthians 12:9). I find the implications of that promise mind-blowing. Living with chronic illness and disability, claiming that promise daily, has become the greatest challenge of my life.... The result has been not happiness, not relief from pain, not ease, but joy. The deepest peace and satisfaction, wholeness and security, in knowing that God is in control of this outrageous situation. Knowing that he holds me in the palm of his hand, and that *nothing* can separate us."

Anne also wrote a song, which makes a powerful prayer:

My grace is all you need,
Today and every day,
My power will make you strong,
You need not be afraid.

My grace is all you need,
The saints have proved it true,
Through fire, torment and death,
They kept their faith in you.

My grace is all you need.
I claim your promise now;
Without you at my side,
Life's a dark and lonely road.

My grace is all you need.
Sometimes almost too much

As joy breaks through the pain
And I feel your healing touch.

My grace is all you need.
In temptation's darkest hour,
At the point of despair,
Then I know your power.

My Lord, my God, my song
Shall never, never end,
And though death may be strong,
Your grace is all I need.

* * *

In a great affirmation of faith, after facing many discouragements and difficulties, St. Paul wrote:

Who shall separate us from the love of Christ? Shall tribulation, or distress, or persecution... No, in all these things we are more than conquerors through him who loved us.

For I am sure that neither death, nor life... nor things present, nor things to come, nor powers, nor height, nor depth, nor anything else in all creation, will be able to separate us from the love of God in Christ Jesus our Lord.

Romans 8:35-39

FIFTY-SIX

We Are More Than Bodies

We are much more than the mass of cells that make up our bodies. Each person possesses depths of being and personality, memories, longings, and creative gifts, with significance far beyond the particular state his or her body happens to be in at any one moment.

Certainly our body, mind, and spirit are intimately linked, and healing is concerned with all three things. But the body is only a part of the whole person, and prayer transcends all bodily limitations.

When we pray for sick people, or for healing for ourselves, we are taken up into the energy of divine love which enfolds us as whole people. Wholeness in Christ is possible without a physically perfect body; and which of us has that anyway?

A FRIEND FROM MY SCHOOL DAYS, Hilary, whose story I often tell, suffered from myasthenia, a rare, muscle-wasting disease. Her body was a wreck, and she lay paralyzed except for her big toe; her tongue hung limply, and her eyes were permanently closed. As an affectionate gesture, and to remind us that this was Hil, a young human being with a sweet nature and a sense of humor, the nurses used to manicure and polish her fingernails.

Hilary communicated with us by operating a highly sophisticated typewriter, "Possum," with her toe. Her conversation, which was always alert and often funny, would appear on a piece of paper at the other end of the small room. Mercifully she was not deaf, so we could talk to her freely. But we were usually tempted to address the typewriter, instead of the person in the bed a few feet away.

Her body showed no sign of life, apart from the mechanical heaving of her chest and the endless click of the ventilator. But the typewritten page was full of her vitality and interest in the world around her.

When we prayed for her, we were holding up to God's love not just a wasted body lying in bed, but somebody who remembered all about us, even though she couldn't see us; somebody who would invite us to look at photographs on the wall of her latest godchildren or nephews and nieces, even though she herself was blind; somebody who teased us ("Twerps!" once appeared on Possum's paper when we misunderstood the name of a German song she was talking about); somebody who was already whole, as a courageous and compassionate person; and somebody who remained faithful to God through her devastating experience.

Hilary taught me something about all of us. God has made us in his image, lovable and able to be loved. The person we are is not confined to our external appearance or bodily condition. Nor is prayer limited to outward, tangible things.

Another friend of mine, Steven, had a rare virus, which paralyzed him for several months. In pain and unable to speak, he was immensely frustrated. Those of us who were praying for him realized that, even though the normal forms of human communication were impossible, the channel of prayer remained unimpaired. Intercession became a way of contact at a very deep level, a way of being with Steven and with God that transcended any physical obstacle.

My father was dying of cancer some years ago, and he knew it. During the final months of his life, my children sent him several homemade get-well cards. On one occasion my seven-year-old son had been learning at school about bones and the structure of the human body. So he decided to make a beautiful card for Grandpa, with a large picture of a skeleton on the front. When he showed me the finished article, I wondered if I could possibly give it to my father. It might have seemed terribly tactless! But, on reflection, I had a strange feeling that it would be all right. So I took the card with me the next day when I visited my father in the hospital.

He opened the card, looked at it carefully, and a large smile spread over his face, such as I had rarely seen since he became ill. And then he roared with laughter. "That's the best portrait I've had done for years!"

I was witnessing something profound beneath all the hilarity. There was a strange new freedom in my father, in spite of all his dreadful suffering. It was almost as if new life was beginning, a glimpse of resurrection in the middle of physical deterioration.

I believe that people's prayers for my father had something to do with this.

FIFTY-SEVEN

Facing the Truth

*We are often afraid to face the truth, especially when some-
one is seriously ill. So we weave a web of lies around the
sick person, adding deceit to deceit. This can lead to the
sort of absurd situation I experienced as a teenager, when
my mother was dying. Everyone knew, but no one would
mention it. I would have given anything to cry freely with
my mother, but the doctor would not allow it.*

*Fortunately, things have changed since then. That was
in the 1960s. More doctors encourage families to grieve
openly together now. In some ways, this is harder to do,
but it does enable you to live and pray with the pain of
truth, not the pain of a lie.*

TELLING PEOPLE ABOUT TERMINAL ILLNESS is a difficult task,
which should be done gently and sensitively. Some people will only come to terms with the truth a step at a time,
while others will want to know everything immediately.
People should be given an honest explanation, so that they
can think and work through their illness, both with their
families and with God.

Some people, however, refuse to face the truth. Much
depends on how they were told and how well they were
supported after receiving the news. I heard recently of a
woman who was informed at an outpatient clinic that she

had cancer. As soon as she stepped out the door, she convinced herself and her family that she was perfectly well. Even when her strength began to fail, she dismissed her illness as "nothing at all." Because she had denied the truth, family members were drawn into the deception and never had the chance to share her pain or grow together during the last few months of her life.

By contrast, an elderly pastor preached a sermon in which he said, "Every night when I go to bed, I lie down and say, 'Into your hands, O Lord, I commend my spirit'—the words of Jesus when he died. I never know whether I'm going to wake up in the morning or not, so you could say I'm having a trial run!"

To be prepared for death is not a gloomy business. On the contrary, readiness for death adds a lightness of spirit, a carefree honesty about the fact that none of us can hold on to our earthly bodies and possessions forever.

Death has become the great taboo in our society; it has replaced sex as the unmentionable subject. People just switch off; they don't want to know. This is a strange way for us to behave, considering the fact that dying is an experience that we will all face one day. The idea of being forced to let go of all that is familiar and dear to us in order to launch out alone into the unknown, appalls many of us. Prayer has an element of dying to self and of uncertainty as well. Perhaps if we prayed more we would fear death less, and be better able to look forward to the "many mansions" which Jesus promised to prepare (John 14:2).

FACING THE PAINFUL TRUTH

In 1987 a woman whose son had died from AIDS a year earlier spoke on television. At first she had refused to believe he was dying, and had been filled with bitterness. The first step toward facing the truth came when she brought herself to rub her son's feet, legs, and back with a form of massage which is particularly comforting to people who are in the advanced stages of AIDS.

When her son died, she swore she would never set foot in the hospital again. But then she realized that making such a vow was tantamount to falling back into denial. So she prayed to be given the courage to look squarely at what had happened.

To her surprise and credit, she found herself returning to the hospital. She began by giving massages to other young men with AIDS and then showing their mothers how to do it. This meant going back into the room where her son, Maurice, had died. It was difficult, but she did it and was all the better for it.

Now this bereaved mother can help other mothers because she understands what they are going through, and she knows how they hide their own pain to spare their sons from seeing it.

She said, "I've learned that you can't walk around fear or pain; you've got to walk right through it. But it's hard, God knows."

He does know, from the inside.

* * *

In this excerpt from Laurens Van der Post's novel, A Story Like the Wind,[21] *the speaker is Ousie-Johanna, the family cook. She is complaining about her employer, Lammie, whose husband, Ouwa, has recently died. Lammie is pretending to be cheerful, and acting as if nothing tragic has happened. Ousie-Johanna says to the son of the family:*

I don't know what is blerrie-well the matter with that Lammie of yours. Why has the good God in heaven given people grief if not to weep over it? Can't she see that she owes it to Ouwa to weep for him? If she's not careful she'll turn him into a ghost that will haunt us.

FIFTY-EIGHT

New Values and Priorities

Facing illness and death, either in ourselves or in other people, can alter our values. Things which used to matter a great deal now pale into insignificance, and we become more aware of how vital human love and forgiveness are. We also start to appreciate ordinary things more fully, and we see the beauty of the world with new eyes.

"A ND LIVE EACH DAY AS IF THY LAST," we used to sing solemnly at school assemblies. This line, from the old hymn *Awake My Soul*,[22] seemed to me then rather morbid. But over the years I have come to see the wisdom in those words.

A friend of our family regularly visits a children's hospice, where she perches on the end of the beds playing her flute. Some of the children are well enough to play a variety of instruments, and parents quickly get involved in the fun of do-it-yourself concerts. Very often, in the middle of death, something comes alive. People discover new creativity and new ways of enjoying things together, because every moment is precious.

Illness can change our priorities. A friend of mine told me

how she felt when her small son had an emergency operation. The day before she had been upset about not finding the right material for curtains and upholstery to redecorate her house. Then her son doubled up with stomach pains and was rushed into the hospital for surgery. She said, "Now I couldn't care less what color the cushions are!"

Prayer is closely related to all this. Living contemplatively means being open to the present moment and being aware of what matters most. It means being inwardly still and empty, in order to perceive the full impact of creation; enjoying but not clinging, gazing but not grasping, living life to the full but dying to self.

All of us are dying! But it often takes the closeness of somebody else's death to make us appreciate the good things which are under our noses—the colors, the smells, the laughter, and the incredible fact that people love us.

Certainly pain and illness can break people. I am not advocating a sentimental and naive view of suffering. But tragedies can also become the seed bed for new growth. If we ask God to make us more alive through our own dark experiences, he will help us. The very fact that we want this to happen makes it possible.

* * *

If this were the last day of your life, ponder with God who you would like to be with and how you would listen to them, who you would want to make peace with, what you would like to look at, and what pleasures you would savor.

Lord, I thank you for the way painful things can sharpen my joy.

FIFTY-NINE

What Have I Done to Deserve This?

It's natural to ask "why me?" when illness, bereavement, or other misfortunes strike. "Why does disease have such power? Couldn't God have arranged things differently?" we ask. "Why should good and generous people suffer so much, while many selfish individuals appear to live in cheerful comfort?"

Simple explanations won't work. Yet one thing is clear: logical standards of what is right and fair do not seem to correspond with the mysterious ways of God.

I RECENTLY HEARD ABOUT A YOUNG COUPLE who went through time-consuming and rigorous interviews in the hopes of adopting a baby. Once they were approved, they had the added strain of uncertainty over whether the baby's natural mother would finally relinquish the child. Eventually the process was complete and the baby was theirs. Two weeks later the baby died of crib death.

That couple must have felt like putting God on trial; it all seemed so utterly meaningless and unfair.

All of us feel like expressing our anger with God at times. When we do so, we may find ourselves asking what we have done to deserve such troubles. But we need to consider the implications of what we are saying when this word "deserve" creeps in.

Our question implies that we favor an exact system of reward and punishment for all our behavior. But try taking this to its logical conclusion for just a moment. What would our fate be if we only got what we deserved? As the writer of Psalm 130 said, "If thou, O LORD, shouldst mark iniquities, Lord, who could stand?" (verse 3). Fortunately the verse goes on: "But there is forgiveness with thee" (verse 4).

If a system of absolute justice governed our fortunes, it is worth pondering what life on earth would be like. The only automobile drivers to be killed would be the ones who had been dishonest or cruel to their families; God would only send rain on the land of virtuous farmers; and so on. Yet Jesus himself pointed out that God is not like that: "He makes his sun rise on the evil and on the good, and sends rain on the just and on the unjust" (Matthew 5:45). If God is not like that, life in his world is not like that either.

What about the men, women, and children who are ravaged by earthquake and famine? Have they directly deserved all their misery? If not, why should I, and not they, be rescued from suffering? If we are determined to apply it, the principle of deserving is a two-edged sword. In reality it is a non-factor. We are given and forgiven infinitely more than we deserve. That is the message of the gospel.

Maybe you have lived your entire life for God, and a cruel illness has hit you. This is not a matter of punishment but of mystery—the mystery of suffering. The only answer we have been given is the cross—the most unfair thing of all. Along with it comes the exuberant certainty that Jesus is alive beyond all pain and death.

* * *

Job, who faced great anguish and misfortune, spoke these words:

> "I loathe my life;
> I will give free utterance to my complaint...
> I will say to God,....
>   let me know why thou dost contend against me.
> Thy hands fashioned and made me;
>   and now thou dost turn about and destroy me.
> Oh, that I knew where I might find him,
>   that I might come even to his seat!
> I would lay my case before him
>   and fill my mouth with arguments."

The Lord answers Job out of a whirlwind:

> "Where were you when I laid the foundation of the earth?
>   Tell me, if you have understanding....
> Have you entered the storehouses of the snow...
> Is it by your wisdom that the hawk soars...?"

Job replies:

> "I know that thou canst do all things,
>   and that no purpose of thine can be thwarted....
> Therefore I have uttered what I did not understand,
>   things too wonderful for me, which I did not know."
>   **Job 10:1-2, 8; 23:3-4; 38:4, 22; 39:26; 42:2-3**

How can you prove a man who leads,
   To be a leader worth the following,
   Unless you follow to the death?
...I have to choose. I back the scent of life
   Against its stink. **G.A. Studdert Kennedy (1883-1929)**
                        Woodbine Willie[23]

SIXTY

Even Christians Get Depressed

"You're a Christian—things shouldn't get you down! Pull yourself together." Such bullying is both cruel and misguided. Who ever said that followers of Christ should live in a permanent state of happiness? Or that so-called "good Christians" never get depressed?

Jesus himself endured the deepest desolation imaginable, and men and women of God ever since have faced periods of darkness. We need to take a far gentler approach.

FEELING WEARY AND FED UP is nothing to be ashamed of. Sometimes, we have to learn to treat ourselves as gently as God does. We need, in fact, to be able to love ourselves. To say this can sound as though I am recommending that we wallow in self-pity or that we condone our sin. But loving ourselves involves accepting the truth that we are of infinite value to God, however unlovable we may feel. After all, Jesus told us to love our neighbors *as ourselves;* he never said that we should hate ourselves.

When life is hell, your true friends stick by you. They listen, they understand, and they take you seriously. They don't make you feel guilty or scold you for feeling the way you do. As a result, you feel free to tell them exactly how things are. Though they may gently try to help you realize what your hurt and unhappiness are doing to you, they will love you through it all.

God is like that. The prophet Hosea sees him as a father, tenderly teaching a small child to walk, and picking him up when he falls down (Hosea 11:1-4). Elsewhere God is described as a mother-hen sheltering her chicks beneath her wings (Psalm 91:4; Matthew 23:37).

Depression makes us acutely aware of our own nothingness, so we have no alternative in prayer but to reach out to God in sheer dependence. The point where our own resources run out is the point where his begin, and we have to cling to him through thick and thin.

Praying when we feel sad or depressed will not necessarily make us feel better. But by doggedly continuing to say, "Lord, I am yours," or "Jesus, help me," or some such phrase, our sadness has at least become part of prayer, rather than something which alienates us from God.

The journey through darkness is one that we share with Christ, although it takes an act of sheer faith on our part to affirm that. Even Jesus experienced "Godlessness," in a moment of desolation on the cross that we can hardly begin to fathom: "My God, my God, why hast thou forsaken me?" (Matthew 27:46). Jesus has already descended into hell. We are not alone, even though it may feel as though we are.

* * *

Lord, now thou hast reduced me to nothing,
I wait on thee to make something of me.
I don't know what.
You have brought me so low, there is nothing
I want to do or be,
but I wait on thee. **Richard Harries**[24]

Prayer can flow into music, and music can flow into prayer as a channel of God's healing power. King Saul in the Old Testament was relieved of dark and melancholy moods whenever David played the harp for him (1 Samuel 16:14-23). One way of praying when we feel sad or depressed is to play something gentle and beautiful, like the slow movement of Mozart's 3rd Violin Concerto (K299). We can read a Scripture passage at the same time. Here are a few you might want to try:

"… My steadfast love shall not depart from you,…
     says the LORD, who has compassion on you.
O afflicted one, storm-tossed, and not comforted,…
     … with everlasting love I will have compassion on you,
     says the LORD, your Redeemer." **Isaiah 54:10-11, 8**

"…I have loved you with an everlasting love…
I will restore health to you,
     and your wounds I will heal, says the LORD.
I will satisfy the weary soul,
and every languishing soul I will replenish."
Jeremiah 31:3; 30:17; 31:25

Other music you might want to listen to includes:
Brahms: Violin Concerto in D. 1st movement.
Brahms: German Requiem. Especially the 5th movement with chorus and soprano: *Thee I will comfort as one whom his mother comforts (Ich will euch troten, wie einen seine Mutter trotet).*
Faure: Requiem, especially the *Sanctus* and *Pie Jesu.*
Mozart: Andante for flute and orchestra in C. K315.
Mozart: Concerto for flute and harp. K299. 2nd movement.
Mozart Clarinet Quintet in A. K581. 2nd movement.

Mozart: Piano Concerto in C. No. 21. K467. 2nd movement.

Mozart: Piano Concerto in F. No. 11. K413. 2nd movement.

Mozart: Clarinet Concerto in A. 2nd movement.

(Most of the second movements are slow and meditative; it can be especially therapeutic to play on to the livelier third movements.)

SIXTY-ONE

Depression

As I write this, I am not feeling the least bit depressed. But there have certainly been times in the past when I've struggled with depression. I remember how difficult it was to relate to the kindly advice given to me by people who hadn't a clue what I was feeling. Only those who spoke out of their own experience of darkness could help.

So I have looked up my old journals, to see what I wrote during the bouts of mild depression that I suffered some years ago. I reproduce some excerpts in the hope that first-hand thoughts, struggles, and prayers, which were then intended for no eyes but mine, may offer some hope to anyone who is feeling depressed.

THIS AWFUL, DULL ACHE around the solar plexus....
I alienate the people I love most. I'm prickly about everybody's response to me. I dread meeting anyone outside, and I resent any demands made on me.

I know I irritate and hurt people. I can see how it happens, but I can't stop it. It's as if I need to vent my feelings on someone—or something.

I'm getting upset over such trivial things. But what aches inside isn't just these immediate things; it goes much deeper. It feels like a swamp of misery underneath....

I must resist the temptation to cut people by words or unkind silences. I must open up my wounds to Christ.

Don't stand still. You are journeying through a desert, and your survival depends on your determination to keep moving.

This entry comes some months later:

Back again in this heavy cloud. Each time the stripping seems to be more painful.

After a talk with Father N., I do believe this can be used as intercession for other people going through hell—and in some sort of dying to self.

I need to be more quiet with God. Pour out my darkness into the love which is streaming from the cross, like a Carmelite in silent adoration of Christ crucified.

Offer it all to God, so that he can transform and take up my pain into his redemptive suffering in the world.

Lord, I plunge into you, and I bring my depression with me. I'm giving you the depression because it's all I've got to offer at the moment.

It's still mine, I'm still feeling it—but it's yours as well....

It feels as if everyone loathes me. But people's opinions of me can't hurt me without my consent.

I will not be ruled by the desire for approval, which gets blown up out of all proportion when I'm like this.

What matters most? My own ego doesn't matter a scrap. Yet it's my ego that lurches around when I feel like this, coloring everything I do with insidious self-pity.

Lord, free me from this tyrant of self.

I don't matter.

Yet I do matter to you. You love me. There's freedom
    in that.

Lord, let me be God-possessed,
  love-possessed,
    instead of self-possessed.

From the following year:
> Empty, miserable and dreary.
> Heavy and lifeless
> In the darkness with God.
> God is more than darkness. Life is more than this.

... This depression is like a huge wave. Lord, help me to ride on it: don't let it engulf me. However awful I feel, nothing can stop me from praying, nothing can stop me from loving, unless I freely choose to let that happen.

Operation depression:
1. Face it squarely
2. Pour it all out before the cross
3. Keep very still
4. Abandon everything I am to God
5. Look Jesus in the eye
6. Stop self-hatred—he loves me
7. No more rushing to the cookie jar for comfort
8. Do something practical, and endure the pain like a toothache.

Next day:

This is hard work. Much easier to slump back into a cushion of misery.

* * *

Lord, give me strength for the effort of each moment as it comes.

SIXTY-TWO

Gifts

One of the most wretched effects of depression is that we lack the energy or initiative to do anything, respond to anyone, or enjoy any part of God's world. Being told to "snap out of it" only makes matters worse.

Yet there is something we can do ourselves in the battle against inertia. We can make the effort, however difficult, to look at and listen to the things immediately around us. If we can do this, new possibilities open up for God to touch and help us when misery looms large, often through the smallest fragments of his creation.

THE GREAT DUTCH CHRISTIAN, Corrie ten Boom, was held in solitary confinement in the Nazi concentration camp at Ravensbruck during the Second World War, because she and her family had given shelter to Jews. In her cell she found immense comfort, even joy, in the presence of an ant. It was another living thing, made by God, just as she was.

I had almost put my foot where he was one morning as I carried my bucket to the door, when I realized the honour being done me. I crouched down and admired the marvelous design of legs and body. I apologized for my size, and promised I would not so thoughtlessly stride about again.

229

After a while he disappeared through a crack in the floor. But when my evening piece of bread appeared on the door shelf, I scattered some crumbs, and to my joy he popped out almost at once. He picked up a heroic piece, struggled down the hole with it, and came back for more. It was the beginning of a relationship.[25]

Most of us do not face that sort of persecution. But Corrie's experience can help us when we are feeling discouraged and unhappy about something. If we are alert, a similar gift of hope may land at our feet.

This concept may sound a bit unrealistic and sentimental: "If you're down in the dumps, all you have to do is look at little birds and pretty flowers, and you'll feel just fine!" Such an approach is nothing but ludicrous.

In the first place, it takes a considerable effort of will to come out of ourselves and appreciate the natural world when we are feeling depressed.

Second, enjoying nature will not automatically make us feel ten times better. Yet we will find a new ingredient added to our experience, if we can summon the energy to be attentive to the natural world.

I once made a list of things I have tried to remember to enjoy, in the struggle to counterbalance the misery of depression. I don't expect that everyone else will find delight in the same things; my aim is simply to give an illustration of what I have been saying.

A smooth pebble, picked up on the beach, with the most beautiful shape and color.
The cat's soft fur and long tail.
Van Gogh's painting of a lark above a cornfield.
The color and texture of—yes!—a cauliflower.
The flame-like leaves of trees in autumn.
The smell of good soap, particularly a kind I often use,

which is made by blind people.

Pink and apricot sunsets.

The song of the chaffinch and the willow warbler.

I am sure that if someone had simply told me I ought "to look at this or listen to that," I would have said yes to them on the outside and no on the inside. Depression makes it hard for us to even want to accept help or to consider new ideas from anyone else, however good they may be; we have to discover things for ourselves.

God deals with each of us differently. All that he asks is that we be ready and open to receiving what he offers us, here and now. This means making space around the particular things which catch our attention—not forcing anything, but just seeing what happens.

* * *

Sometimes our pain actually increases when we look at lovely things. Men who fought in Europe during World War II have said how the beautiful wild flowers of France added to their sense of the futility of war.

But for someone like Mother Julian of Norwich, the great fourteenth-century English mystic, creation's small things give an assurance of the eternal love of God. She, too, lived at a time of upheaval and darkness:

And he showed me more, a little thing, the size of a hazelnut, on the palm of my hand, round like a ball. I looked at it thoughtfully and wondered, "What is this?" And the answer came, "It is all that is made." I marveled that it continued to exist and did not suddenly disintegrate; it was so small. And again my mind supplied the answer, "It exists, both now and forever, because God loves it." In short, everything owes its existence to the love of God.[26]

Are we willing to:

> See with our eyes,
> hear with our ears,
> understand with our hearts,
> and turn and be healed? **Based on Isaiah 6:10**

SIXTY-THREE

A Theology of Tiredness

When we are worn out, and our own resources are nearly spent, the only prayer possible is simply to let go into God. Exhaustion brings into focus our inner poverty and total dependence on him. Relying on ourselves is no longer a temptation; it's an impossibility.

T IREDNESS COMES IN MANY DIFFERENT FORMS.
One type of tiredness has an exhilarating effect which you can experience when things are going well, at work or in other areas of your life. Busy family events can have the same effect, so that you feel you are riding on the crest of a wave, tired but happy. Then prayer is not so much an offering of weariness as of thankfulness.

Such exhilaration, however, is usually followed by fatigue. I remember a retreat weekend in our church, in which we had very little sleep the first night because of excited children and sleeping in strange beds. The next day went well, but breakfast on the final morning arrived with many of us feeling tired and befuddled.

I wondered how on earth I was going to be able to lead my small group. But a wise friend pointed out to me that a "theology of tiredness" is a gateway to trust in God. Does it all depend on us?

Another kind of tiredness comes when life is going badly: people are difficult, work is draining, you have personal problems to contend with. At such times your resilience is low, and you are likely to explode if someone is unkind or doesn't seem to understand you.

Jesus' invitation to lose your life in order that you may find it (Mark 8:35) takes on a new dimension when you are as tired as this. You are so worn out that you have nothing within yourself to draw on. Prayer means surrendering yourself into God's hands and losing your strength and ability in his. All you have to offer him is your emptiness.

At such times, short prayers, like "Jesus: my weariness into your strength," are invaluable.

Perhaps the most common type of tiredness is a mixture of happiness and weariness. We are busy with numerous commitments, and enjoy being involved in many things. But if fatigue and pressure get the better of us, we snap. This always seems to happen when we least want it.

About seven-thirty at night is the time in our house when our children are tired and most in need of my patience and love. But by this time my own resources are at a low ebb, and my temper is easily frayed. Then, the only way I can pray is to say under my breath, "Lord, this is yours," or "Jesus, live in me." I cannot handle my weariness and the chaos around me on my own; all I can do is to give the whole situation to him.

* * *

Why are you cast down, O my soul,
  and why are you disquieted within me?
Hope in God; for I shall again praise him,
  my help and my God.... Psalm 42:5-6

SIXTY-FOUR

No Time for Quiet

It can be terribly frustrating to have no solitude and little opportunity for quiet prayer. But the very fact that we wish we had more time to pray reveals our inner desire for God; and that is important, because reaching out to him is at the heart of praying.

Perhaps all we have to offer him at this particular point is our lack of time. Even this can become a prayer of wanting God, or a "dart of longing love," to use the classic phrase.[27]

YOU ARE TIRED AND OVERWORKED, with a pounding headache. People are being difficult, interruptions abound, and you long to be able to get organized and have some peace. Frustration like this makes God seem pretty remote.

At times, most of us are tempted to think of the demands and chores that clamor for our attention as irritations to be endured. Once these are out of the way, we assure ourselves, we will be able to start really living, praying, and serving God. The busier we are, the more we tend to think like this.

Ask yourself how often the word "just" comes up in your thinking or conversation. "I'll *just* do these jobs before I start thinking about God"; "Let me *just* get through this difficult

235

time, and then I'll be able to concentrate on being a better Christian." Such thinking indicates that we are building escape-routes out of the present moment into some imaginary, ideal future that we will never reach.

The truth, of course, is that we have nothing but the present moment, and it is here that God is waiting to meet us. Everything we do can be given to God, without exception.

This makes sense in theory, but it is difficult to put into practice when we are facing endless work, exuberant children, guests at home, and a lawn that needed mowing last week. If we are honest, living prayerfully is an ideal toward which we are moving, rather than a goal we usually achieve. But some things will help us come closer to that vision.

Something we can do, early in the morning, is deliberately to consecrate the whole day to God. Then it's done, whether or not we remember to turn to him regularly throughout the day.

Sometimes it helps to identify some sort of object as a symbol of our basic desire to live all our life rooted and grounded in God. One of my favorites is a Celtic cross on a chain, which I wear as a necklace. Another is an icon of Jesus. Such a picture, painted while the artist was praying and fasting, points beyond itself to Christ who is present with me throughout the day.

Water is another great symbol of Christ. I know someone who uses the following prayer when she first turns the faucet on in the morning: "Living Water, cleanse me, and be a spring of eternal life welling up within me."

A single word or phrase can also become an invaluable companion during the day. One prayer that always helps me when I am feeling harassed and tempted to tear my hair out is simply, "Lord, this is yours." I like this prayer because it is deliberately ambiguous. The word "yours" can mean "coming from you" or "given to you," and I want to express both those things.

There will never, of course, be time to *do* very much! What we are able to accomplish will depend to a great extent on the opportunities and resources which God gives us. But there will always be time to pray, because all time can be prayed in.

I know a man named Martin who is a night nurse in a geriatric hospital. He comes home exhausted, and even after sleeping finds it a struggle to do anything with his family or to do much around the house. He is a Christian, and is involved in many activities at church as well.

At one time he was depressed because he wanted to draw closer to God, but felt that his prayer life was in a shambles. He did manage to spend five minutes with the Bible each day, but couldn't seem to do much more. He described what it was like at night during the long hours on duty:

> Sometimes a dozen things happen at once and it's bedlam; but there are long stretches when it's very still and quiet. I do feel near to God then. You're close to life and death, and there's something awesome about that. I often feel that God is there when someone is dying. Sometimes it's awful—the mess and the smells, and some of the people can be very crotchety. But I try to do the work for God even when I'm hating it.

Martin was relieved at the suggestion that God was not waiting to add extra burdens to his already demanding life. Perhaps God actually wanted him to *relax* when he came home from work. Martin began to realize that God was already giving him a great deal of material for prayer in the ward at night: intercession, silence, and sharing in the world's pain. His task was to respond to what was already there, not to hunt around for further disciplines to impose on himself.

Days off work were different; there were chances for other

kinds of praying then. But in the hospital Martin only had to recognize the possibilities for prayer which were right under his nose.

* * *

Many ancient Celtic prayers capture the essential truth that all of life is God's life and is contained in his love, and that every activity can become prayer. The hymns and prayers intermingle mundane and heavenly things with a disarming simplicity. In her booklet God under my Roof [28] *Esther de Waal quotes some poems sung by women in the mornings:*

> *I will kindle my fire this morning*
> *In the presence of the holy angels of heaven...*
> *God kindle Thou in my heart within*
> *A flame of love to my neighbour...*

Another is a farmer's prayer:

> *I will go out to sow the seed,*
> *In the name of him who gave it growth...*

There are also many journey-prayers, for example:

> *Bless to me, O God*
> *The earth beneath my foot,*
> *Bless to me, O God,*
> *The path whereon I go.*

"Life is only for loving. Time is only that we may find God."

St. Bernard

SIXTY-FIVE

Too Much to Do

Either you fight against a demanding schedule, or you sur-render to the flow of it. Constant demands can seem like a treadmill, dreary and draining. But by positively accepting every task and interruption as it comes, you can become less bound by a sense of compulsion. A job that was forcing itself on you becomes something you freely do, the object of your wholehearted attention.

S AYING YES TO THE PRESENT MOMENT can involve a kind of dying to self. Plans for a peaceful evening must take sec-ond place to the needs of other people; the desire for a clean house must wait, while we seize an opportunity to be quiet with God. We may even have to abandon our time of quiet and solitude with God, in order to deal with a child in need.

Letting go of the many other things we would rather be doing and giving all our attention to the task in front of us is a positive act of limitation, for love's sake. It is a form of obedience.

DECIDE AND DO

Sometimes we have so much to do that we're at a loss about which job to tackle first, and we don't know when to take a break. It would be so much easier if God would tell us what to do, step by step, so that we could simply obey without thinking.

Praying and agonizing about each decision can become ridiculous. So the motto "decide and do" is useful. I find it best to survey the possibilities as quickly as I can, offer my will to God, and then make the decision, doing my best to abandon my preoccupation with other things on the list.

A POSITIVE VIEW OF INCOMPLETENESS

Completing jobs and projects can become an obsession for us. And we forget that the present moment is never complete. If I am sowing seeds, I cannot harvest the vegetables at the same time. I can, however, be wholly given to the particular part of the process in which I am involved today.

Prayer, too, is always incomplete, because it is essentially a longing for God, not a possessing of him. We are always journeying into a deeper relationship with God. We have never completed our praying. So our frustration when we have to cut our prayer-time short in order to go to work or cook a meal can be transformed into a shaft of desire for God, which is itself a particularly valuable form of praying.

* * *

Peace must always exist in the midst of our imperfections....
Imitate the calm of the sailor standing on the deck of his ship.

Abbé de Tourville [29]

Lord, you put twenty-four hours in a day;
you gave me a body which gets tired and can only do so
    much.

Show me what you want me to do,
   and how you want me to pray.
Help me to
   Open my eyes and look;
Taste what I am eating;
Listen to what I am hearing;
Face what I am suffering;
Enjoy what makes me laugh;
Celebrate the ways I am loved;
And offer what I am doing,
So that the water of the present moment
   may be turned into wine.

SIXTY-SIX

I'm Not Sure
I Want to Pray!

When ten or twenty minutes fall into our laps, God is offering us a gift. Nobody wants our attention, no commitment requires our presence, and no task is urgent. We actually have a space in which we could sit still and be alone with God. This is the moment that tests our priorities. Are we willing to let go of all the other things we would like to be doing?

TO BE HONEST, we often feel reluctant to pray, and for a variety of reasons. For instance, we may be feeling the pull of a half-decorated bedroom or an unopened newspaper. Or we may be tempted to escape into a swirl of activity because we are afraid of what God might ask of us. In that case, we are saying no to prayer because we do not want to be too exposed to God, too vulnerable to the cost of discipleship.

But God never asks the impossible of us. He only draws us toward what we are capable of doing with his help. In other words, he enables us to become our real selves—and to find true happiness in the process.

When we do settle down to spend time with God, we may have to begin simply by offering him our reluctance to pray.

Even if we're not reluctant, we experience an inner resistance to changing gears in the middle of a hectic day. Our minds will probably run on with numerous distractions. But that won't matter as long as we stay put.

On a practical level, I find it helpful to light a candle, as a way of saying to God, "This flame won't go out. It is a sign that I *want* to be open to you during this period of time, even though I may wander off into numerous distractions." Repeating a prayer such as, "Spirit of Jesus, breathe on me," is a way of moving into the stillness underlying the noise which daily life usually imposes upon it.

With the candle lit, ask Christ to melt you into himself, so that you may become increasingly absorbed in the love and silent presence of God our Father.

Many Christians will agree that the more we make space for God, the more he makes himself known to us.

* * *

"Anyone who prays knows the connection between the "yes" which is expressed and, to some extent, diluted in the affairs of daily life, and the "yes" spoken neat in prayer." **Maria Boulding**[30]

Jesus said, "Be like men who wait for their master's return from a wedding-party, ready to let him in the moment he arrives and knocks. Happy are those servants whom the master finds on the alert when he comes" (Luke 12:36-37, NEB).

SIXTY-SEVEN

A Special Kind of Cross

Buried in the rubble of a street in Canterbury for eleven hundred years was a small cross which looks like this.

T HE WAY EACH ARM OF THE CROSS opens right out can be seen as a symbol of all our praying through the pain and shadows of our lives.

The upward movement represents our reaching out to God in trust, opening our whole being to him, often in emptiness and darkness: "Into your hands, O Lord, I commend my spirit" (Psalm 31:5).[31]

The downward thrust stands for God pervading the hidden depths of our being. It also conveys our need to be rooted and grounded in God, come what may: "In him we live and move and have our being" (Acts 17:28).

245

The cross beams stand for our experience of the world. The more we pray, the more exposed we become to the pain of other people, and the more aware we become of God's activity through suffering, both in our everyday life and in the wider world. Prayer also opens our eyes to the miracle of creation.

Each arm opens out eventually into infinity, the unfathomable, silent presence of God who is in and beyond all things.

God is also at the center of the cross, in Jesus, who entered the heart of all our sin and misery, and redeemed it from the inside.

So this Canterbury cross can be a symbol of all our praying and longing and suffering with God.

On the four small triangles on each beam, there is a typically interwoven Celtic pattern. This is a reminder of the intimate connection between the things of God and everyday life, a link which is reflected, as we have seen, in much Celtic poetry.

* * *

Thomas Becket, Archbishop of Canterbury, stood in his cathedral on December 29, 1170, and turned to face the king's knights as they burst in to murder him.

This was his supreme yes, a yes to death, but also a yes to God's life in him. It was a yes reached through prayer and inward struggle, an acceptance made possible by Christ's own yes on the cross.

Somehow we too have to stand still, face our shadows, and become pain-bearers with Christ.

Peace,
These things had to come to you and you accept them;
This is your share of the eternal burden,
The perpetual glory. **Words of Thomas à Beckett to the distraught women of Canterbury just before his death**[32]

Notes

Introduction

1. Quoted in *The Lord of the Journey*, ed. Pooley and Seddon (Collins, 1986), p. 351.

Part One:
Praying with Your Hurts

1. *Marked for Life* (SPCK/Triangle, 1985), pp. 63-4.
2. Source unknown.
3. "Little Gidding" 1.206, *Four Quartets* (Faber, 1970).
4. *Yes to God* (DLT, 1975), ch. 3, p. 50.
5. In *The Oxford Book of Prayer*, ed. George Appleton, OUP, 1988.
6. Constance Babbington Smith, *Iulia de Beausobre: A Russian Christian in the West* (DLT, 1983) p. 134; also referred to in Iulia de Beausobre's *Creative Suffering* (Fairacres Publication No. 88, 1984), pp. 16-17.
7. Quoted in *Lord of the Journey*, ed. Pooley and Seddon (Collins, 1986), p. 349.
8. *Letter from Taizé*, May-June 1986.
9. *The Listener*, 24 October 1946, p. 555.
10. Adapted from a prayer by Jim Cotter, in *Prayer at Night*, 4th edition (Cairns Publication, 1988), p. 50.
11. These words were found scribbled on a notepad on the desk of a parish priest, soon after his death.
12. Translated from the Russian, in *Pencil Letter* (Bloodaxe Books, 1988).

13. Prue Wilson, *My Father Took Me to the Circus* (DLT, 1984), p. 22.
14. CMS magazine, *Yes*, May-June 1988.

Part Two:
Praying with Your Sinfulness

1. Available on *Your Hundred Best Tunes*, New Chart, vol. 3, Decca SPA 565 (or cassette KCSP 565).
2. See also the music for praying with low spirits on page 151.
3. *The English Poems of George Herbert*, ed. C.A. Patrides (Everyman/Dent, 1974), p. 192.
4. Gerard Hughes, *God of Surprises* (DLT, 1985), p. 117.
5. Iago to Othello, *Othello* Act III, iii. 1.169 William Shakespeare (Collins, 1968).
6. Source unknown.
7. Roald Dahl, *James and the Giant Peach* (Puffin, 1961), pp. 32-33.
8. *Thoughts in Solitude* (Burns & Oates, 1987), p. 24.
9. Philippa Craig, *Living from Within* (Grail, 1979), p. 22.
10. In Leslie Houlden (ed.), *A Celebration of Faith* (Hodder & Stoughton, 1970), p. 200.
11. From *Prayer Is My Life* (USPG, no date).
12. *Praying Round the Clock* (Mowbray, 1983), p. 105.
13. (Fairacres Publication No. 88) pp. 13-14.
14. This idea of reducing a text to certain key phrases and words is fully explored in *Towards Contemplation: A Practical Intro - duction for Prayer Groups*, by Peter Dodson (Fairacres Publication No. 64); see also his *Contemplating the Word* (SPCK).
15. "Silence in Prayer: the Meaning of Hesychia" in M. Basil Pennington (ed.), *One Yet Two: Monastic Tradition East and West* (Cistercian Studies Series No. 29), p. 31.
16. Quoted by Sister Edmée in *Silence in Prayer and Action* (Fairacres Publication No. 78).
17. *Listening to God and Listening to Community* (Fairacres Publication No. 69).
18. On a Christmas card, adapted from a prayer by the late Bishop of Bloemfontein.

Part Three:
Praying with Misfortunes, Fears, and Frustrations

1. *A Doorway to Silence* (DLT, 1968), p. 3.
2. Father William Barry, "Wrestling with God," *The Tablet* 11 April 1987.
3. Ibid.
4. From *Heiligenstadt Testament* (1802), translated by Alfred Kitchin.
5. *Seeds of Contemplation* (Anthony Clarke Books, 1961), p. 204-6.
6. *Moment of Christ* (DLT, 1984), p. 62.
7. (SPCK, 1983), pp. 10-11.
8. From a prayer card by Spes Sancta, Newbury.
9. *Thoughts in Solitude* (Burns & Oates, 1975), p. 21.
10. Talking on BBC Television, "The Cost of Discipleship," February, 1988.
11. *Heaven in Ordinary* (Mayhew McCrimmon, 1985).
12. *Praying Round the Clock* (Mowbray, 1983), p. 54.
13. He was released on December 3, 1989. For more information about Soviet Christians in prison, contact "The Vigil," c/o Rev. Dr. Dick Rogers, 63 Meadow Brook Road, Birmingham B31 IND, UK.
14. *Oxford Book of Prayers* edited by George Appleton, p. 284.
15. From *Prayer Is My Life* (USPG).
16. Dom John Chapman, *The Spiritual Letters* (Sheed & Ward, 1938), p. 25.
17. The prayers are to be found on pages 9 and 25. The motifs are on pages 9 and 15. Published by Triangle, 1985.
18. David Adam, *The Edge of Glory* (SPCK/Triangle, 1985), p. 49; the motif is on p. 87.
19. For example, TZ 405 *Cantate*, TZ 408 *Resurrexit*. Production by Presses de Taizé (distributed by Auvidis).
20. BBC Radio 4 "Sunday" 27 September, 1987.
21. (Penguin, 1972), p. 436.
22. Written by Bishop Thomas Ken (1637-1711).
23. From the poem "Faith" in *The Unutterable Beauty* (Hodder & Stoughton, 1964).
24. *Praying Round the Clock* (Mowbray, 1983), p. 101.
25. *The Hiding Place* (Hodder & Stoughton, 1971), p. 144.

26. *Revelations of Divine Love,* ch. 5, translated by Clifton Wolters (Penguin, 1966).
27. Anon., *The Cloud of Unknowing,* translated by Clifton Wolters (Penguin, 1961), ch. 6.
28. (Fairacres Publication No. 87), pp. 13, 18, 17.
29. *Letters of Direction* (Dacre Press, Westminster, 1961), p. 81.
30. *Marked for Life* (SPCK/Triangle, 1985), p. 5.
31. Drawing by Sister Theresa Margaret CHN in Joyce Huggett's book *Open to God* (Hodder & Stoughton, 1989), p. 85.
32. From the play, *Murder in the Cathedral* by T.S. Eliot (Faber, 1965), Part II, line 246ff.

Acknowledgments

I AM GRATEFUL TO FR. WILLIAM BARRY, SJ, for permission to refer to his article "Wrestling with God" in *The Tablet*; also to Clare Amos for permission to quote her article about weeping and prayer in the CMS magazine *Yes*; to Dame Cicely Saunders, DBE, for permission to quote two excerpts from a BBC Radio 4 "Sunday" interview, September 27, 1987; to Dr. Jean Vanier, for permission to quote his interview on the BBC television program "The Cost of Discipleship" in February 1988; to the Rev. David Adam for permission to use the motifs from his book *The Edge of Glory*; to Sister Theresa Margaret, CHN, for permission to use her drawing from Joyce Huggett's book *Open to God*; and to the Dean of Canterbury Cathedral for permission to use the Canterbury Cross in the last section of the book.

Thanks are due to the following for permission to quote from copyright sources:

Anthony Clarke Books, 16 Garden Court, Wheathampstead, Herts AL4 8RF, for the excerpt from *Seeds of Contemplation* by Thomas Merton, 1961.

BBC Publications, 35 Marylebone High Street, London WIM 4AA, for the excerpt from the *The Listener*, October 24, 1946.

Bloodaxe Books for the excerpt from *Pencil Letter* by Irina Ratushinskaya.

Burns & Oates, Wellwood, North Farm Road, Tunbridge Wells, Kent TN2 3DR, for the excerpt from *Thoughts in Solitude* by Thomas Merton, 1975.

The Rev. Jim Cotter, Cairns Publications, 47 Fifth Park Avenue, Sheffield S5 6HF, for the excerpt from his book *Prayer at Night,* 4th edition, 1988.

The Church Missionary Society, Partnership House, 157 Waterloo Road, London SEI 8UU, for the excerpt from an article by Clare Amos in the magazine *Yes,* May-June 1988.

Cistercian Publications Ltd., WMU Station, Kalamazoo, Michigan 49008, USA, for the excerpt from *One Yet Two: Monastic Tradition East and West,* ed. M. Basil Pennington (Cistercian Studies Series No. 29).

Wm. Collins & Co. Ltd., 8 Grafton Street, London W1X 3LA, for the excerpt from Shakespeare's *Othello* in the *Complete Shakespeare,* 1968; for the excerpts from *Lord of the Journey,* ed. Pooley & Seddon, 1986; and for the excerpts from the Book of Common Prayer [no date given].

Darton, Longman & Todd Ltd., 89 Lillie Road, London SW6 1UD, for excerpts from *Yes to God,* by Alan Ecclestone, 1975; *Iulia de Beausobre: A Russian Christian in the West,* by Constance Babbington Smith, 1983; *My Father Took Me to the Circus,* by Prue Wilson, 1984; *God of Surprises* by Gerard Hughes, 1985; *A Doorway to Silence* by Robert Llewelyn, 1986; and *Moment of Christ* by John Main, 1984.

J.M. Dent & Sons Ltd., Aldine House, Albemarle Street, London, for the poem *Love III* by George Herbert, ed. C.A. Patrides, Everyman, 1974.

Faber & Faber, 3 Queen Square, London WC1N 3AU, for the excerpts from the *Four Quartets* by T.S. Eliot, 1970; *Murder in the Cathedral* by T.S. Eliot, 1965; and for the excerpt from the Puffin Book *James and the Giant Peach* by Roald Dahl, 1961.

The General Synod of the Church of England, Church House, Dean's Yard, London SW1P 3NZ, for excerpts from the Psalms in *The Alternative Service Book,* 1980.

Grail Publications Ltd., 125 Waxwell Lane, Pinner, Middlesex, for the use of a story from *Living from Within* by Philippa Craig, 1979.

Hodder & Stoughton Ltd., Dunton Green, Sevenoaks, Kent TN13 2YA, for the excerpt from *A Celebration of Faith,* ed. Leslie Houlden, 1970; for the excerpts from the poem "Faith" in *The Unutterable Beauty* by G.A. Studdert Kennedy, 1964; and from *The Hiding Place* by Corrie ten Boom, 1971.

McCrimmon Publishing Co. Ltd., 10-12, High Street, Great

Wakering, Essex SS3 OEQ, for the excerpt from *Heaven in Ordinary* by Angela Ashwin, 1985.

A.R. Mowbray & Co. Ltd., St. Thomas House, Becket Street, Oxford OX1 1SJ, for the excerpts from *Praying Round the Clock* by Richard Harries, 1983; and *Letters of Direction* by the Abbé de Tourville, 1939 Dacre Press, A. & C. Black Ltd.Oxford and Cambridge University Press, The Edinburgh Building, Shaftesbury Road, Cambridge CB2 2RU, for the verses from The New English Bible, 2nd ed., 1970.

The Oxford University Press, Walton Street, Oxford OX2 6DP, for the excerpt from *The Oxford Book of Prayers*, ed. George Appleton, 1985.

Penguin Books Ltd., 5563 King's Road, London SW19 OUH, for the excerpts from *A Story Like the Wind*, by Laurens Van der Post, 1972; *Revelations of Divine Love* by Mother Julian of Norwich, trans. Clifton Wolters, 1966; and *The Cloud of Unknowing*, trans. Clifton Wolters, 1961.

SLG Press, Convent of the Incarnation, Fairacres, Oxford 0X4 1TB, for the excerpts from *Creative Suffering*, Pub. No. 88 by Iulia de Beausobre; *Silence in Prayer and Action*, Pub. No. 78, by Sister Edmée; *Listening to God and Listening to Community*, by Mother Mary Clare, Pub. No. 69; and *God Under My Roof*, Pub. No. 87, by Esther de Waal.

The Society for Promoting Christian Knowledge, Holy Trinity Church, Marylebone Road, London NW1 4DU, for the excerpts from *Marked for Life*, by Maria Boulding, 1985, and *The Edge of Glory* by David Adam, 1985, both Triangle Books; also *Beyond All Pain* by Dame Cicely Saunders, 1983.

Spes Sancta, Newbury, for an excerpt from a prayer-card, quoting Rev. Mother Stuart.

The Tablet, 48 Great Peter Street, London SW1P 2HB, for the excerpt from an article by Father William Barry, SJ, "Wrestling with God," 11 April 1987.

71250 Taizé Community, France, for the excerpt from *Letter From Taizé*, May-June 1986.

The United Society for the Propagation of the Gospel, Partnership House, 157 Waterloo Road, London SE1 8UU, for the excerpts from *Prayer Is My Life* by Margaret Dewey (date not known).